"If we learn by doing, then this book will go a long way towards helping the reader "do the right thing," In every case, Plante's lucid and succinct explanations of ethical approaches and principles are followed by an imaginative set of exercises that immediately test those approaches and apply those principles to real life situations. The book is not a formulaic set of answers, but an explanation and exploration of methods—their strengths and weaknesses—to help the reader live ethically."

—Stephen A. Privett, SJ, president,
University of San Francisco

DO THE RIGHT THING

Living Ethically in an Unethical World

THOMAS G. PLANTE, PH.D., ABPP

New Harbinger Publications, Inc.

Publisher's Note

This publication is designed to provide accurate and authoritative information in regard to the subject matter covered. It is sold with the understanding that the publisher is not engaged in rendering psychological, financial, legal, or other professional services. If expert assistance or counseling is needed, the services of a competent professional should be sought.

Distributed in Canada by Raincoast Books

Copyright © 2004 by Thomas G. Plante
New Harbinger Publications, Inc.
5674 Shattuck Avenue
Oakland, CA 94609

Cover design by Amy Shoup
Cover image © Digital Vision/Getty Images
Edited by Brady Kahn
Text design by Tracy Marie Carlson

ISBN 1-57224-364-3 Paperback

Printed in the United States of America

New Harbinger Publications' Web site address: www.newharbinger.com

06   05   04

10   9   8   7   6   5   4   3   2   1

First printing

Dedication

To my maternal grandfather, the late Henry George McCormick, who taught and inspired me to always strive to do the right thing.

The life which is unexamined is not worth living.

—Plato

Contents

PART 2
Five Ethical Principles to Guide All Decisions

PART 3
Living the Ethical Life

Acknowledgments

Many people other than the author assist in the completion of a book project. Some contribute in a direct way while others help in a more supportive manner. I would like to acknowledge the help of the many people who worked to make this book a reality.

First, I'd like to thank the wonderful people at New Harbinger who published this book. Dr. Matthew McKay initially approached me with the idea after he attended one of my ethics workshops for mental health professionals at Santa Clara University's Center for Professional Development. Many thanks to Jueli Gastwirth, Melissa Kirk, Heather Mitchener, Tracy Carlson, Troy DuFrene, and Brady Kahn.

Second, I would like to thank a variety of people and places that have helped me with the book project and the ethics courses and workshops that I have taught. These include the Markkula Center for Applied Ethics at Santa Clara University (Professor Kirk Hanson, Director) for its support and assistance in funding this book project. I'd also like to thank Professor David Perry, who reviewed and commented on several chapters, student research assistants Ryan Bogden, Kamran Khan, and Martha Belo for helping with the research for the book, and the many psychology students who have taken my ethics classes at Santa Clara and Stanford universities, offering ideas, challenging questions, and insightful comments about all things ethical. I would also like to thank Santa Clara's Center for Professional Development and the psychology department (especially Henrietta Matteucci and Patricia Brandt) for help with the book and with my classes in ethics. Thanks also to the department of psychiatry at Stanford, which has allowed me to teach ethics for its psychiatry and psychology trainees. Thanks also to Rabbi Janet Marder from Congregation Beth Am (Los Altos Hills, California) and Professor Thomas Sheehan at Stanford for their help with a number of biblical and other sacred text references.

Third, I would like to thank the various ethical models in my life, including Henry and Anna McCormick, Margaret Condon, Mary (Plante) Beauchemin, Lee (Plante) Sperduti, Marcia (McCormick) Plante, John Sousa, Frs. Sonny Manuel, Steve and John Privett, Paul Locatelli, and Patrick Labelle, as well as Dr. Peter Merenda and both Eli and Marilyn Goldfarb.

Finally, I would like to thank my wife Lori and son Zachary for their love and support while I worked on another book project and for their fine example of ethical living and problem solving. They make everything worthwhile, assist me in living a life worth living, and reminding me about what is most important in life.

PART 1

Why Use an Ethics Approach to Decision Making?

Introduction

"How should I live my life?" This is probably the most fundamental question that we can ask ourselves. What are the values and principles that you use to determine how you interact with others and go about your day-to-day activities? For some people, living a good life means living a life in pursuit of pleasure and riches. For these people a good life is perhaps a life of selfishness, getting all that they can out of the experiences and opportunities that come their way, with little regard for others. For most people, however, living a good life is about more than money, self-centeredness, and hedonism. Most people find selfish pleasure-seeking ultimately empty and unsatisfying (Myers 2000). Most people value honesty, fairness, integrity, love, competence, and concern for others. Although they would certainly enjoy more money and pleasure, they know that a life worth living involves something more. In this book, I'll try to show you how living an ethical life can lead to living a good life.

Here's a scenario to make some of these issues come to life. Suppose you were nominated to run for a high political office. You might be very excited. Perhaps you had hoped for this moment throughout your life. All of a sudden, people from all walks of life are interested in your life story. Reporters begin asking people who've known you over the years to comment on their experiences with you. They interview your elementary school teachers, former boyfriends and girlfriends, neighbors, coworkers, and even people who hardly knew you at all before but who are speaking about you anyway now that you're famous and in the news. How would you react? Are there things you have said and done that would trouble you if they became public? Would you be upset to watch reporters interviewing certain people from your past? What might these people say about you?

Imagine another scene. Suppose your entire life has been video-taped. Not one second of your life has been left out. You might remember the popular movie *The Truman Show,* starring Jim Carey, which highlighted this very situation. Say someone who doesn't like you very much has a copy of this videotape and wants to carefully review it for scenes that would embarrass you. They're motivated to put you in a highly unfavorable light. They'll edit the videotape and show it to the world. What scenes would you be worried or morti-fied about others seeing?

These scenarios illustrate that living a good life and one that you can be at peace with might involve living an ethical life. Living an ethical life means doing the right thing on a regular basis even when faced with really tough dilemmas and decisions.

How Do You Do It?

Doing the right thing isn't always so simple, is it? Trying to do the right thing raises many questions. Is there really a "right thing"? How do we do the right thing if there is one? What's the right thing for me? Is my right thing different from your right thing? What if I don't want to do the right thing? What are the odds that doing the right thing will make my life better?

These are difficult questions, but they must be addressed if you're to have any chance of finding principles and strategies that will help you live a life that you can be satisfied and at peace with. You must try to find answers, even if complete answers aren't possi-ble. The attempt to address these questions will result in your being better equipped to navigate a life that is ultimately more satisfying, even if it can't be perfect.

The fact is, we all have some idea or conception about living a good life. We all have some idea about how we should go about being in the world. You may have instincts about these issues that aren't fully thought out or articulated. The development of a more careful and useful process to think through these questions is likely to result in a better and a more satisfying life, as well as in better decision making.

Life is full of decisions. Whether they are big or small, they all have ethical implications if you are thoughtful and careful enough to look at them though an ethics lens. You may think that ethics only concerns the big societal questions of our day such as euthanasia, abortion, corporate greed, cloning, and capital punishment. Ethics is also involved with many life decisions that we routinely face. Here's a short list of some ethical questions that people typically confront.

> Should I leave my spouse when I have fallen in love with another person?

> Should I save money for my children's education, or shall I spend extra money on myself?

> Should I use plastic or paper bags to carry my groceries?

> Should I continue to work at a job I enjoy when the organization that I work for is not making the world a better place?

> Should I follow orders from my boss that would result in me doing unethical things?

> Should I take the opportunity to save money by cheating on my taxes?

> Should I give money to a homeless person who is begging on the street?

> Should I stop and help someone having car troubles on the freeway?

> Should I give CPR to a disheveled stranger on the street who has vomited after experiencing a seizure and is not breathing?

> Should I tell the waitperson at a restaurant that an error was made in my favor on a dinner bill?

> Should I risk my welfare to help someone else in need?

These and other similar questions are common examples of challenging decisions that you might face. How would you answer these questions? What guidelines would you use to handle these situations?

The Purpose of This Book

The purpose of this book is to try and help you manage questions such as these that emerge in daily living. The book will propose a step-by-step decision-making strategy using five ethical principles to handle both small and large life decisions in your personal and professional life. It will then focus on ways to build ethical muscle by finding ways to use these ethical principles to make good decisions about really hard life issues. This book should help you develop your own sense of ethics based on your core values and beliefs about the way your life should be lived.

Looking at Small and Big Ethical Decisions

It's important to look at small issues as well as big issues. How can we expect to make solid ethical decisions about really difficult and challenging dilemmas if we can't make good ethical decisions regarding small matters? How can we engage in dishonesty in small matters (accepting too much change from a store clerk) and then expect to be totally honest in something really big (cheating on taxes or cooking the books in a large company)? Learning to make good ethical decisions in small ethical dilemmas will help you make good ethical decisions in really tough situations. If you can see most of your daily decisions as potentially ethical decisions and if you can feel comfortable using some strategy to filter and guide your decision making, then you will be in a much better position to make solid ethical decisions when the issues get tough.

Is Living an Ethical Life Realistic?

Can you succeed in a global economy and in life in general by always making ethically sound decisions? Is being ethical also being naïve and a chump? Some people think so. A recent study found that 50 percent of American workers admitted to unethical behavior at work and cited stress and job pressures for their unethical behavior (Ethics Officer Association. American Society of Chartered Life Underwriters and Chartered Financial Consultants. 1997). Is living an ethical life unrealistic in contemporary society?

American culture sends mixed messages on this topic. On the one hand, the culture tends to value the common good, compassion, and altruism, yet we also value independence, success, and being number one. Look at what mixed messages we send to our young children in this area! We encourage preschool and elementary school children to share their toys, help others, be kind, and be a good sport. Yet we also encourage them to win on the sports field, get top grades, and stick up for themselves. Face it, making good ethical decisions can be very challenging and can cost you a lot. Doing the right thing can sometimes be a hard path to follow.

At the same time, ethical behavior can, more often than not, increase your success, and following an ethical path is often consistent with doing well. For example, if you were cheated by someone or by some business, would you ever trust this person or business again? If you are caught in a lie, what are the odds that the person who caught you will ever believe you again? Doing the right thing not only helps you to live with yourself but often results in good things happening to you in the long term. Thus, doing the right thing will often result in more life satisfaction. Doing the right thing is good for you (as well as for others). Of course, there are occasions when doing the right thing can have upsetting consequences (losing a job or lots of money). However, in the long run, life satisfaction is likely to be higher even when doing the right thing results in short-term disappointment.

A skeptic might ask, "Who needs ethics?" He or she might say, "I'll do what's right for me in the moment." If we look around us, it often appears that many people will make decisions that are in their own best interest, regardless of the ethical implications of their decisions. Many people appear to be motivated by wealth, power, fame, and pleasure, and not by ethics. Reading the daily news headlines certainly reinforces this impression. For example, a CIA employee sells sensitive military secrets to another country for money while a female nurse marries a stranger on television for fame and fortune. Someone embezzles money from their employer or elderly parent while a wealthy celebrity shoplifts items that they could afford to buy. A business executive lives an extravagant lifestyle while employees from his or her company are being laid off or paid below a living wage. The news seems to suggest that we're motivated to make decisions not based on ethics but based on greed and self-interest.

Leaving ethical decision making to impulse is not a great idea. In the moment, we may make either good or poor decisions. If we've given some thought to strategies for making ethical decisions in our day-to-day experiences, then we're more likely to consistently make good decisions. As the saying goes, "Don't shop when you're hungry." Thinking that you'll make good spontaneous ethical decisions in the moment when you're challenged is unrealistic. You need to be thoughtful to maximize the odds that you'll do the right thing when you need to.

By the Way, Money Really Can't Buy Happiness

Money, power, and fame really can't buy happiness, though you wouldn't know it by observing many people's behavior. According to an annual UCLA survey of college freshmen, "being very well off financially" was "very important or essential" to 44 percent of students in 1965, but that number has steadily increased, reaching 75 percent of students in 2000 (Myers 2000). It's curious to note that while prosperity has significantly increased during the past fifty years, self-reported levels of happiness have stayed the same. The data is dramatic. For example, while inflation-adjusted personal income has almost tripled since 1956, the percentage of Americans reporting that they are "very happy" has remained steady at 30 percent during the past forty-five years (Myers 2000).

On the one hand, we're privy to so many modern conveniences, technological and medical advances, good economic times, and increased personal wealth. On the other hand, national levels of depression, anxiety, and stress remain the same. Curiously, as countries around the globe increase their economic prosperity, levels of depression (especially among youth) increase. So, it appears clear that making decisions based on what profits you the most is unlikely to result in happiness and may ultimately be unsatisfying. Having the most money may not ultimately satisfy us. We need something else to be satisfied.

How Ethical Dilemmas Have Changed

In some ways, ethical dilemmas are very different today from what they were in the past while in other ways they're the same. Some difficult ethical decisions that we're faced with weren't possible years ago. Technological and medical advances create ethical dilemmas that were unheard of just a few short years ago. For example, using the Internet to view pornography or to obtain confidential information about others wasn't possible before the Internet was readily available to the public. Using medical technology to determine the gender and genetic health of fetuses has only recently become available to pregnant women. This information can then be used to decide to terminate a pregnancy. Changes in social norms and customs also have created potential ethical dilemmas that didn't exist years ago. For example, parents have more choices or decisions about who will raise their children (family members or hired help) than they did in previous generations. So, as science, technology, culture, and society have changed, so have many of the ethical dilemmas that many people face.

Other ethical issues really haven't changed much. For example, people have been having affairs since the dawn of time. Marital infidelity has been an ethical issue ever since marriage existed. Choosing to lie and cheat has also been an ethical issue down through the ages as well. There are many ethical dilemmas today that have been with us for as long as humans have walked the earth.

Although many of these issues haven't changed in recent years, our way of thinking about them has changed a great deal. For example, for many centuries, rules for behavior adopted by particular religious traditions made the differences between right and wrong very clear. Issues such as marital infidelity, cheating, lying, stealing, and so forth had strict rules outlined by clergy and church groups. Furthermore, deviation from many of these rules resulted in severe consequences, including death. Yet, many people may have secretly disagreed with the rules. The point is that civic and church groups throughout the ages have tried to outline exactly how we should live our lives. As society has become more secularized, more options for behavior and living our lives have become available. With this freedom came the responsibility to decide for ourselves how we should live. While most people welcome the personal freedom to choose how to live, they then have the obligation to make important ethical decisions for themselves rather than relying on church or civic groups to tell them how to behave.

Finally, ethics (or the lack of ethics) has received a great deal of national and international attention in recent years. The collapse of major American companies such as Enron, World Com, Arthur Anderson, Tyco, and others has highlighted the remarkably unethical behavior of some top executives. The sexual abuse of children by Catholic priests and other clergy, as well as the poor manner in which Church leadership managed these sex offending clergy, highlights unethical behavior among our supposed moral and ethical leaders. Furthermore, cheating, lying, lack of integrity, greed, and other problems in so many segments of society highlight the lack of good ethical behavior on the part of so many people. Certainly, people have behaved in unethical ways throughout history. But mass media has broadcast incidents of unethical behavior across the globe.

In some ways, we're indeed faced with different ethical dilemmas than we were years ago. In other ways, we're faced with the same dilemmas, but they have a different twist due to societal changes as well as societal norms and expectations.

Avoiding Ethical Help

Ethics basically attempts to answer the question, "How shall I live my life?" Ethics is a set of principles for living and decision making. Ethics is also a discipline of critical reflection on the meaning and justification of moral beliefs. Why do so many people avoid ethics? There are several common misconceptions. These include

1. Ethics means strict rules of behavior.

2. Ethics and religion are too closely connected.

3. Ethics is obvious.

First, many people see ethics as being a list of firm rules of behavior. People generally dislike being told how to behave and value the freedom to act as they see fit. Attention to ethical guidance may be perceived as giving up some personal freedoms to follow a list of dos and don'ts. Using ethical principles to guide decisions doesn't have to follow strict rules of behavior, however. Rather, these principles can guide and inform your decision making and not necessarily control you or make you feel guilty if you choose to behave in a particular way.

Second, many people see ethics and religion as being very closely connected. Those who don't gravitate towards an organized and structured religious tradition may avoid ethical guidance because they see it as too closely interconnected. Many see religious or ethical guidance as being hypocritical because they feel that clergy who espouse these rules don't necessarily follow them. Many high-profile clergy members (Jesse Jackson, Jimmy Swaggart, Jim Bakker) who frequently instruct others on how to live in an ethical manner have been found to be guilty of not following their own advice.

Again, the Catholic Church has received a great deal of attention regarding priests who sexually abuse children. While any sexual abuse of children is horrific, the fact that the abuse was perpetrated by supposedly celibate Catholic priests from a Church that stresses very high expectations regarding sexual behavior from its members appears especially hypocritical. Thus, many people who witness such behavior among religious and moral leaders may avoid ethical guidance from them.

Finally, many people think of ethical guidance as being straightforward and obvious, and therefore, they don't feel that it is needed. They may think of ethical principles, such as being honest and fair, as something they try to achieve as best as they can. They also may feel that especially egregious examples of unethical behavior (spying for another country, embezzlement of company funds, lying in court) are activities that they'd never engage in and thus they don't feel they need any guidance in these areas.

Once they get started, however, most people seem to appreciate and enjoy conversations about ethical decision making. Furthermore, being better able to think through problems and dilemmas using helpful ethical principles will more likely result in good decision making. Better decisions will hopefully result in an improved ability to live the kind of life that you'll feel good about; making good ethical decisions will lead to more life satisfaction, better relationships, and a life path that you'll be pleased with.

A Positive Approach to Ethics

This book isn't about dos and don'ts. This book won't be preachy. This book won't try to instill in you a sense of guilt for not making noble and ethical decisions. It will outline options for ethical decision making that are based on solid research and a clinical understanding about how people can make good, ethical, and hopefully satisfying decisions for themselves. There may be many times in this book when the answer to an ethical dilemma may not be clear, or several reasonable and even contradictory conclusions could be made. The book will focus on ethical principles to filter your thinking so that you can increase the odds that you'll make good decisions for yourself. Will you make good ethical decisions all the time after reading this book? Probably not. However, you'll likely have a better understanding and sensitivity to ethical issues that emerge every day and have reasonable and practical guidelines for solving them.

How This Book Will Help You

This book is different than most other books on ethical decision making. First, I am a clinical psychologist who regularly grapples with ethical decisions with clients in a psychotherapy practice. Psychotherapy is one place where people truly say what's on their minds and in their hearts and thus provides a window into the challenging ethical dilemmas faced by people each day. I also teach ethics to undergraduate psychology students at Santa Clara University, to graduate students, interns, and postdoctoral fellows in psychology and psychiatry at Stanford University, and to mental health professionals in Northern California. These experiences have helped me to better understand how people deal with ethical questions on a daily basis. I have designed this book to be practical, with numerous examples and exercises for the reader. The book uses an easily followed and remembered step-by-step approach for making good ethical decisions. Too often, people may read a self-help book that feels useful when they are reading it but that is hard to implement after they've finished reading. This book focuses on ways to maintain and maximize ethical decision making long after you have completed reading this book.

Chapter 1 details nine different approaches to ethical decision making that come from the wisdom of moral philosophers throughout the centuries, as well as various religious traditions. The review highlights the fact that there are many different ways to approach ethical decision making and that each approach may result in different answers to ethical questions. After this review, the chapter will outline a five-step process for making ethical decisions, regardless of which approach to ethics you want to use. Then, it goes on to introduce five ethical principles to live by. Finally, the chapter will end with a strategy for you to develop your own core ethical values using these five principles as a base.

The goal of chapter 2 is to help you understand how almost every daily decision can be considered an ethical decision if you look closely enough at the problem. This chapter will sensitize you to the ethical issues that you face with every decision and interaction. It will help you develop a more sensitive and fine-tuned ethical gut.

Chapters 3 through 7 will focus on each of the five ethical principles introduced in chapter 1. These chapters seek to help you better understand and appreciate how each of these principles can be applied to almost any daily ethical decision.

Chapter 8 will focus on how you can develop ethical muscle to make challenging decisions long after you put down this book. This chapter will help you develop strategies to cope with the downside of making good ethical decisions as well. Behaving ethically can cost you in some ways, and so finding ways to live ethically, even when there are negative consequences, is needed to build ethical muscle.

Finally, chapter 9 will review what you have learned in this book and discuss resources that you might use to maximize good ethical decision making in the future. Chapter 9 answers the question, "Where do you go from here?"

As you read on, I recommend that you use a journal to record your thoughts. Keeping a journal will increase the chances that you will fully integrate these important concepts about ethical decision making into your life. On that note, please don't gloss over the suggested exercises, but complete them and record your responses in your ethics journal.

Do the Right Thing

My maternal grandfather, Henry McCormick, died of congestive heart failure at the age of ninety-two on January 1, 1993. I remember visiting him in a Pawtucket, Rhode Island nursing home a few days before he died. It was clear that this visit would be our last, and as I got ready to leave, he had some final words for me that included three requests. The first was "take care of your grandmother." His ninety-two-year-old wife of seventy years was also living in the nursing home but was in relatively better health. The second request was "pray to the Virgin Mary." He was a devout Irish Catholic who attended Mass each day. His third request was "always do the right thing." This final request speaks to the importance of living an ethical life. My grandfather knew that doing the right thing throughout your life gives you peace in the end.

In my many years as a practicing psychologist and university professor teaching classes on ethics, it has become clear to me that most people benefit from thinking about strategies to best live their lives. People don't necessarily set out to make unethical decisions. Many good people make bad decisions. People seem to need more guidance in this area as church and civic groups have steadily lost their influence. Over the years I have developed a way to think through ethical dilemmas that has been helpful to my clients, students, and associates. This experience inspired this book. I suppose that my grandfather's request to "do the right thing" also motivated me to think about the right thing and try to share some of the fruits of that thinking with you.

Ethical decision making is a reasonable way to approach the many decisions and issues that we face in life. Following an ethically informed life path will maximize the odds that you'll lead a satisfied life and will be at peace knowing that at least most of the time you did indeed do the right thing.

CHAPTER 1

Approaches to Ethics

There is more than one way to peel an apple. There are often many different and productive ways to accomplish the same goal. In an effort to make good ethical decisions, we can use different strategies. There are a variety of ways to think about ethics. There are different frames of references and perspectives that can help guide us. There isn't just one correct approach. Furthermore, different approaches to ethics can be used for different questions or even the same question. You can try to answer an ethical question by examining the reasoning behind several ethical approaches.

This chapter, will review several ways that moral philosophers and ethicists think about ethical issues. After introducing each approach, you'll be asked to complete an exercise to determine how useful that approach is to you. This will help you develop a solid foundation for ethical decision making.

While the list below is not exhaustive, it highlights nine common ethical approaches. Some of these approaches overlap; they aren't meant to be independent or orthogonal. They're meant to be nine reasonable ways to think about ethical issues.

As you read about each ethical approach, think about whether it appeals to you or not. Think about the types of situations in which each approach might (or might not) be helpful to you. Think about which approach resonates with you and your life.

If you're interested in learning more details about these approaches beyond what will be discussed in this chapter, you may wish to read *The Elements of Moral Philosophy*, by James Rachels (2003). It's an excellent and very readable book detailing the approaches highlighted in this chapter. Rachel's book is especially good for the lay reader. Other books on ethics are listed in the resources section.

After discussing each ethical approach and applying it to some ethical dilemmas, this chapter will outline a five-step strategy for facing ethical questions. The five-step process can be used with any of the approaches to ethics discussed and should be considered when facing ethical decisions big or small.

Cultural Relativism

Everything is relative. You've likely heard that phrase. It's a helpful way to understand and remember the cultural relativism approach to ethics. The idea here is that an ethical decision, or the right thing to do in any given situation, might be closely related to a specific culture or context. Cultural traditions, experiences, and expectations create rules for behavior. What might be ethical in one cultural tradition might be unethical in another tradition. Acceptable behavior in one group might be unacceptable in another. Therefore, when trying to make ethical decisions, it's important to take into consideration the cultural context of an ethical question or issue.

Limits of Cultural Relativism

Cultural relativism has its limits. Recently, a great deal of press attention has been on the plight of women in fundamentalist Islamic countries. It was reported that women weren't allowed to work, receive medical care, or even expose their face in public. Reports of routine physical abuse and neglect of women who held no power or control in the Taliban government frequently appeared in the press. While this treatment of women might be generally accepted as appropriate behavior among a particular subculture of Islamic fundamentalists, many would argue that it's not ethical behavior regardless of the cultural context. Other ethical principles such as basic human rights (that will be discussed later in this chapter) might be used to trump or override cultural relativism.

This important limitation of cultural relativism is an excellent example of why you can't merely choose one ethical approach and ignore the rest. While you should understand and evaluate the various approaches to ethical decision making discussed in this chapter, you'd be hard-pressed to say it's entirely ethical to completely ignore the ones you don't like. So, if the Taliban said that it's indeed ethical to treat women poorly because of cultural relativism, many people would likely disagree and say that all humans, regardless of cultural or religious traditions, are entitled to basic human rights.

Cultural Relativism and You

In a nutshell, cultural relativism is a reminder that ethical and other decisions do not occur in a cultural vacuum. Rather, we should take into consideration cultural traditions and expectations when making ethical decisions. Differences in expectations can be based on race, ethnicity, religion, upbringing, or socioeconomic, geographic, or other characteristics.

EXERCISE 1.1

Here's an exercise to help you better understand the influence of your own cultural traditions on your ethical decision making. You may want to write in your journal as you answer these questions.

What is your ethnic, racial, socioeconomic, religious, and geographic identity? How would you describe your background, as well as the background of your family members from previous generations?

Now, what qualities and values would you say are characteristic of people who come from backgrounds like yours?

Finally, how do these qualities and values inform your style of ethical decision making? Are you more individualistic or community oriented, for example? Do you value open expression of feelings and beliefs or a more reserved approach? Do you feel more democratic (let the majority rule) or more autocratic (the head of the family decides) in your decision making?

What have you learned about yourself in this exercise? How does your background influence the way you approach ethical problems? On a scale of 1 to 10, where 1 is "not at all" and 10 is "very," how useful do you think cultural relativism is in helping you make good ethical decisions?

Egoism

If it feels good, do it. Egoism tries to answer the question, "What'll make me feel the best?" Egoism does not appear to be very ethical on the surface—how can trying to feel good be ethical?—however, many decisions based on egoism can indeed be solid ethical choices.

In fact, an egoism approach to ethics is likely to be the one most people use much of the time. When faced with an ethical dilemma, most people probably consider what decision would likely be in their own best interest and thus benefit them in some important way. It's not necessarily egotistical to consider your own self-interest, unless it's the only thing you consider important.

Egoism can be masked in altruism. For example, you might appear to make very altruistic decisions for the benefit of others, but these decisions might be made primarily so that you feel good about yourself. For example, you might hear about children and families starving in various parts of the world. You send money to help them. In doing so, you feel good that you've done your part in fighting hunger. Therefore, while the donation may appear to be a selfless act, in reality it was done to feel good or to relieve guilt.

The motives behind altruistic behavior are usually complex. While feeling good about the altruistic acts might be egotistical, most people who engage in these noble behaviors do so sincerely to help others. Thus egoism may be part but not the entire reason behind selfless or generous acts.

Limits of Egoism

Egoism also has its limits. What's in your best interest might not be in the best interests of others at all. For example, gaining as much material wealth as possible might be in your best interest. You may even justify your wealth by saying that you give a proportion of your income to charity. Yet, your efforts at securing wealth may prevent you from spending time with your children and giving very generously in other ways to those around you. Your efforts to gain wealth could be based on unethical behavior such as lying, cheating, stealing, hurting others, and so forth. Clearly, what makes you feel good will not always be the right thing to do in all situations.

Egoism and You

It is natural and reasonable that you'd consider your best interests when faced with an ethical decision or dilemma. There's nothing wrong with that. However, before you make a decision, it would be useful for you to consider the role of egoism in influencing your thinking. In this way, you'll hopefully be more fully informed about the role of selfish motives before acting on a particular decision or impulse.

EXERCISE 1.2

Here's an exercise to highlight how important egoism might be in your life. Again, you may want to write in your journal as you answer these questions.

What makes you feel good? Do you pride yourself on being a good parent, an employee who is honest and fair, and a generous person with others? Do you volunteer in some capacity? If so, how does volunteerism make you feel? What do you get out of selfless, generous, or kind acts? What do these questions tell you about your motives? Do you act in an ethical manner for the benefit of others, for yourself, or for all parties? Be honest with yourself. Are you likely to behave in an ethical way only if it benefits you? On a scale of 1 to 10, where 1 is "not at all" and 10 is "very," rate how useful you think egoism is in helping you make good ethical decisions.

Utilitarianism

Utilitarianism tries to approach ethical issues by asking what would please the most people. This is a very democratic approach to ethical decision making. When faced with an ethical question, the utilitarian approach would be to try to please the most people involved. Therefore, voting and allowing the majority to decide on an outcome would often be the utilitarian approach.

At first pass, this approach to ethics seems quite reasonable. Voting is a democratic way to help decide questions and solve problems. The approach assumes that people can generally be trusted to make good ethical choices when given the opportunity to vote on the matter. So, when an ethical issue emerges, the utilitarian approach might suggest that those who are affected by the decision vote on a course of action.

Limits of the Utilitarian Approach

Like all ethical approaches the utilitarian approach has its limits. The majority of people could make a decision that isn't very ethical at all. For example, it may make the majority of people happy to lynch a child molester. A majority of people might be pleased if a smug celebrity falls from grace and is humiliated in the press. A majority of people may choose not to do anything to help the homeless in their community. There are many examples where the majority of people might behave in an unethical manner.

Tragically, people in many communities in the United States engaged in racially motivated lynchings during the late 1800s and early 1900s. These horrific events resulted in numerous African Americans being killed by angry mobs. Large numbers of community residents would observe and support these murders. The utilitarian approach would suggest that these lynchings were okay because they made the majority of community members happy. Of course, the person being killed (along with their family and friends) would disagree with this logic. Do you think these murders were ethical?

Here's a tough ethical question: If the same thing happened today, would you speak out against such lynchings if doing so might put your life and the life of your family in danger?

Utilitarianism and You

Living in a country that highly values democratic ideals, it is generally easy for us to debate issues and then vote on an outcome. We do this both formally and informally in our day-to-day activities. Letting the majority rule is a pretty comfortable way of being with others in a democratic society. Therefore, when you're faced with an ethical decision or dilemma, you may wish to consider what will please the majority of people. However, it's important to keep in mind that what pleases the majority of people isn't always the most ethical response. Other factors and ethical approaches must be taken into consideration as well.

EXERCISE 1.3

Can you think of an example in your life where the majority of people voted to do something that you thought was unethical? What happened? How did it make you feel? What did you do? Did you speak up? What other ethical principles were violated? What might you do differently if faced with this situation today? On a scale of 1 to 10, where 1 is "not at all" and 10 is "very," how useful do you think utilitarianism is in helping you make good ethical decisions?

Absolute Moral Rules

The absolute moral rules approach to ethics claims that there are specific rules for behavior that should apply in all circumstances regardless of the consequences. For example, you should always be honest, kind, respectful, generous, and so forth. No one should be allowed to rape or torture children or animals.

Limits of Absolute Moral Rules

While this seems to be a reasonable enough approach, absolute moral rules have important limits as well. Although the famous philosopher Emmanuel Kant was a proponent of absolute moral rules, he offered a wonderful illustration of what many would say are the potential limits of absolute moral rules. Suppose a man ran past you trying to hide from another man chasing him with a knife. The man trying to escape the man with the knife hides and you know exactly where he is. The man doing the chasing asks you where the man is hiding. Do you tell the truth knowing that the hiding man will be killed if found? Do you lie and thus help spare his life? An absolute moral rule, such as "always tell the truth," would encourage you to tell the man with the knife where the other man is hiding, regardless of the consequences.

Honesty is just one of many potentially absolute moral rules. There are many others. For example, absolute moral rules could include that we should always be generous, kind, polite, respectful, and so forth. Again, while on the surface, these ethical rules might seem reasonable or might be useful under most circumstances, there are likely many times when being kind, polite, respectful, and so forth could be unreasonable. For example, should we be kind to child molesters and murderers? While some people might argue that we should show kindness to all people, regardless of who they are or what they've done, others could argue that some people who commit such horrible crimes shouldn't be shown kindness and generosity.

Absolute Moral Rules and You

What do absolute moral rules have to do with you? You likely have certain moral rules that you value and support; for example, you might feel that you should generally be honest. Few people can embrace absolute rules, however. You may, for example, find it reasonable and even ethical to lie under certain circumstances.

EXERCISE 1.4

What are some important absolute moral rules for you? Do you always tell the truth? Are you always kind? Are you always respectful to others? Do you think you should never show anger? Do you have any absolute moral rules? Do you think everything is relative and there are no absolutes?

Come up with a list of five absolute moral rules that you follow. What do they tell you about your approach to ethics? Can you list some examples when you didn't follow your own rule? Why did this happen? On a scale of 1 to 10, where 1 is "not at all" and 10 is "very," how useful do you think absolute moral rules are in helping you make good ethical decisions?

The Social Contract

The social contract approach to ethics suggests that in order for us to live happily in a community, we must utilize both a formal and informal understanding about how we should all behave to best get along. Life would be terribly dangerous and chaotic if people didn't respect a social contract regarding both public and private behavior. Most of our laws are based on this important concept. Laws seek to provide structure and guidelines so that a group of people can live together in a safe and orderly manner. If individuals or a group of people choose to violate an important social contract, then structures are in place to arrest and punish them.

Laws are formal ways to best ensure that people follow important social contracts. They provide consequences for those who might harm others. They prevent people from violating social norms and expectations of behavior. However, there are many more informal contracts that we generally abide by while living in a community. People naturally wait in line to buy movie or subway tickets. If a child you don't know is hurt on a playground and there's no parent or guardian nearby, you'd likely try and comfort and help the child. In order for us to live in the world and get along with others, the idea is that we must each behave in a manner that allows all of us to get our needs met.

Limits of the Social Contract

Like all approaches to ethics, the social contract approach has its limits. First, people may disagree about the terms of the social contract. For example, while avoiding violence and breaking the law may be part of the social contract, many might argue that breaking the law via civil disobedience is indeed ethical. Martin Luther King, Jr. was well-known and respected for his nonviolent approach to breaking laws that were unjust. Some, such as Malcolm X, have argued that violence can and perhaps should be used to right a wrong or to obtain justice. The United States military used violence to destroy the Nazi regime during World War II. While not everyone would agree that the use of military force is ethical, most would argue that the military behaved in an ethical manner based on a "just war" or social contract model of ethics. That model might include the notion that violent and destructive actions against innocent persons must be stopped by any means necessary in order for us to maximize living together in peace.

Reasonable people trying to behave in an ethical manner can certainly disagree about the elements of a social contract. Furthermore, the informal or formal social contract may differ between groups in the same society. Thus, tension is likely to exist since people may not universally agree about what are reasonable and unreasonable contracts.

The Social Contract and You

How might a social contract help you make ethical decisions? How do the rules of society help (or hinder) you in making good ethical decisions?

EXERCISE 1.5

Make a list of the important social contracts you experience in your life. What social contracts do you think are most useful? Are there social contracts that you feel are unreasonable or unjust? Why? On a scale of 1 to 10, where 1 is "not at all" and 10 is "very," how useful do you think the social contract approach is in helping you make good ethical decisions?

Rights Approach

The rights approach to ethics suggests that every human being has certain rights that should be protected and promoted. For example, many people in America agree that people have a right to express their opinion even if it's unpopular. Americans also value the right to "life, liberty, and the pursuit of happiness." Many feel that as long as you harm no one, you have the right to think and behave as you like. Some argue that every human should have the right to food and housing. Some feel that everyone should have the right to some job that pays a livable wage. Everyone may feel that there are rights that all humans are entitled to have and pursue, but reasonable people may disagree about what exactly is on this list of rights.

Limits of the Rights Approach

Of course, there are limits to the rights approach to ethics as well. For example, do people have a right to have sexual feelings for children? Do people have a right to purchase child pornography? Do people have the right to hold strong racist beliefs? Is it ethical to believe that all members of a minority group are lazy or unintelligent? Is it ethical to believe that only members of your particular religious tradition are correct and all other members of various religious traditions are wrong? Should someone who is lazy but able to work have the right to food and housing? Should someone who wishes to commit suicide be able to do so?

It's possible to make this more concrete. The United States has generally been supportive of equal rights for both men and women. Most Americans as well as citizens from Canada, England, and many other industrialized countries would agree that men and women should be entitled to the same rights and responsibilities. However, some countries do not allow women to work, obtain medical care, vote, or even show their face in public. Many people argue that our view of ethics should be imposed on others and that we should work to change these oppressive policies in other places. Others suggest that we should not impose our will in these areas. What then is the ethical response to countries, cultures, and communities who don't share our view of equal rights for both men and women?

Rights and You

How does the rights approach to ethics impact you? You probably have some opinion about what rights people should be entitled to. How do you think this impacts your ethical decision making?

EXERCISE 1.6

Make a list of what you consider to be basic human rights. Consider this your own bill of rights. What do you think all humans should have a right to have or do? List them.

What does your list tell you? Do you think that most people would agree with your list? Why or why not? Do you think your list is reasonable for any culture or country? Why do you think people should have the rights that you listed? On a scale of 1 to 10, where 1 is "not at all" and 10 is "very," how useful do you think the rights approach is in helping you make good ethical decisions?

Justice Approach

The justice approach to ethics highlights what's fair. The justice approach focuses on treating others in a fair, reasonable, and respectful manner. It suggests that the rules and laws of the land apply to all regardless of position, status, power, wealth, and so forth. While the justice approach sounds reasonable and likely to be endorsed by most people, justice is often hard to come by in many different issues that we face. Take the issue of employment. While the justice approach might suggest that all job applicants should be treated fairly and that the best qualified person should get the job, those who are blessed with attractive looks and social skills generally are able to get many benefits in life, relative to those who are thought of as unattractive and not socially skilled or shy. In fact, much research in social psychology has demonstrated that people usually find attractive people more intelligent, wise, talented, sophisticated, and generally possessing a halo effect. Thus, an attractive person is more likely to get a job, be allowed to bend rules, and receive other privileges relative to unattractive people. Is this fair? Is this just?

Limits to Justice

The justice approach, like all of the approaches to ethics, has limits. In addition to the issue raised above, we may also ask, what exactly is meant by justice. Some might find it unjust that anyone, regardless of the reasons, should be homeless or without a meal. Some might find that it is unjust that any employee would make significantly more money than another employee would. For example, the famous Vermont ice cream company, Ben and Jerry's, once had a rule that no one in the company (including the CEO or president) could make more than seven times the salary as the lowest paid worker. Some would argue that it is unjust to spend money on things that are not truly needed (fancy clothes, cars, toys, vacations, meals) while others are starving and homeless. Thus, there are as many different ways to define justice as there are people to discuss and debate this topic.

Justice and You

Whenever you hear or say the refrain, "that's not fair," you know you've hit upon a justice-related issue. How does the justice approach to ethics impact your ethical decisions?

EXERCISE 1.7

How do you define justice? What would a just community look like for you? What would you be willing to give up to build a more just world? What do your answers tell you about your view of justice and ethics? On a scale of 1 to 10, where 1 is "not at all" and 10 is "very," how useful do you think the justice approach is in helping you make good ethical decisions?

Common Good Approach

The common good approach to ethics states that what's in the best interest of the community is what's most ethical. Therefore, if it's in the best interest of the community to imprison child molesters, then it's ethical to take away their rights to freedom in order to protect the greater community. The common good approach might suggest that it's important to use tax monies to feed the homeless because it's in the common good to be sure that everyone has enough to eat.

The common good approach is especially evident in cultures and communities that highly value collaborative and collective approaches to society. Cultures and communities that focus more on individual rights and freedoms, such as in the United States, may experience conflicts with many of the common good approaches. For example, it would be in the best interest of our society for people to eat a healthy diet, not smoke or drink alcohol to excess, and always practice safe sex. A healthier population would mean longer life for many and less money being spent on expensive health care costs. However, most Americans would likely oppose any limitations placed on their personal freedoms to eat, drink, smoke, and be sexual as they see fit. Therefore, although most people might agree that living a healthier lifestyle would be in the best interest of all, few would welcome limitations on their freedoms.

Limits of the Common Good Approach

As in all approaches to ethics, the common good approach also has its limitations. Not everyone would agree with what is the common good. Some might suggest that allowing homosexual partners to adopt children isn't in the common good. Others might argue that religious fundamentalism, regardless of religious tradition, isn't in the common good. Still others might suggest that allowing abortions isn't in the common good. Of course, many others would vigorously support the opposite position of these examples. Therefore, reasonable people might disagree with the criteria for the common good. Furthermore, even if we could all agree on the criteria, ethical dilemmas would still emerge. For example, it's in the common good for all airplanes to ensure that terrorists not be allowed to board an aircraft. However, the way we ensure that this happens might create challenging ethical dilemmas. Should racial profiling be used to screen airline passengers since most recent terrorists have been young men from the greater Middle East?

Common Good and You

How does the common good approach impact you and your ethical decision making? It is often challenging to behave in a way that advances the common good rather than your own needs. For example, SUVs are very popular in the United States but they get very poor gas mileage and can hurt or kill others more easily during a traffic accident. While it might be in the common good for people to refuse to drive SUVs, few people who own them would give them up, based on the common good.

EXERCISE 1.8

Make a list of the things that you could do to advance the common good. What could you do to minimize pollution, save power and other natural resources, and help the community? Once you complete your list, circle the items that you think you would actually do differently for the benefit of the common good. How many items, if any, did you choose? On a scale of 1 to 10, where 1 is "not at all" and 10 is "very," how useful do you think the common good approach is in helping you make good ethical decisions?

Virtue Approach

The virtue approach to ethics suggests that there are a number of qualities or personal characteristics that we value and should all strive toward, such as honesty, integrity, responsibility, compassion, politeness, thoughtfulness, kindness, competence, and so forth.

Most people would likely agree with a core list of virtues that all members of society should strive toward. We'd hope that everyone is honest, responsible, thoughtful, caring, kind, civil, generous, loyal, friendly, courteous, and so forth. These are values that we encourage our children to adopt and that we usually seek in selecting friends, coworkers, and relationship partners. We expect these virtues to be supported by employers, government officials, church leaders, and many other areas of our society.

Limits of the Virtue Approach

There are several challenges with a virtue approach to ethics, however. First, can we all agree on a list of virtues that we should strive towards? For example, some people highly value politeness while others think that it's overrated. Secondly, under what circumstances should we express these virtues? For example, you would expect yourself to show kindness, compassion, and understanding to young children, friends, and your spouse, but would you expect to express these qualities with Nazis or child molesters? Finally, it may be unreasonable to expect that these values can be expressed in every circumstance. For example, there are occasions when being dishonest might be the more ethical choice. For example, if you were dealing with someone who wants to kill all the members of a particular group, and you and your children were members of this group, would you be honest with this person about who you are?

Each culture, community, and religious tradition may have its own slant on the list of virtues to strive towards, and different individuals might feel strongly about some but not all of these virtues. Furthermore, agreeing on a set of virtues is one thing; being motivated to follow them is another. You could be skilled in ethical analysis and support ethical principles in theory, yet have no commitment to do the right thing when you're personally faced with an ethical dilemma.

Virtues and You

What do virtues have to do with your ethical decision making? Whether you've thought about this or not, you likely have some sense of virtues that you think are honorable or worthy of pursuit.

EXERCISE 1.9

Think about all of the virtues that you admire. List as many virtues as you can think of. Then circle the five virtues that you think are especially important. Can you rank them in terms of importance to you? Are these virtues that you highly value in others? On a scale of 1 to 10, where 1 is "not at all" and 10 is "very," how useful do you think the virtue approach is in helping you make good ethical decisions?

What Works for You?

Of the nine approaches to making ethical decisions, which approach or approaches appealed to you the most? Look over your ratings for each of the approaches to determine which approaches you feel most (and least) comfortable with using. Review the approaches you feel most comfortable with using. As you face both small and large ethical dilemmas, you may wish to first consider the approaches you feel most comfortable with and see where those approaches lead you in your decision making. You can use as many of these approaches as you like. However, you are likely to use the approaches that appeal to you most.

Five Steps to Making Ethical Decisions

Each of the approaches discussed in this chapter can help guide your decision making. But how? When making ethical decisions, you might want to look at the dilemma from various points of view. For example, suppose you are trying to decide if you should call in sick to work. You're not really sick, but you want to take a sick day. You are thinking of lying by telling your boss that you are physically ill. Is lying justified? you might ask yourself. What you plan on doing with your free time might impact how you view the ethical issues involved with the decision. For example, if you were going to the beach to soak in sun and fun, then you might view the ethics very differently than if you were going to attend a memorial service for someone you knew well.

This example illustrates that the ethical approach you take would partially depend on the reasons for your behavior. Regardless of which approach or approaches you choose to use, you'd likely benefit from using the following five-step process to think through your ethical dilemmas. This model has been used in numerous environments and has been adopted, by the Markkula Center for Applied Ethics at Santa Clara University. Every ethical issue can be examined through this five-step model.

Step One: Recognize an Ethical Issue

First, you must recognize that there is an ethical or moral issue at hand. If you're attentive to it, you'll likely see ethical issues emerge on a daily basis. In fact, it could be argued that almost every decision and interaction with others is an opportunity to make an ethical or unethical choice. We're constantly faced with decisions each day that challenge us. For example, suppose your boss asks a question which you feel like you should know the answer to, but you don't. Do you lie and try to fake a good response, or do you tell the truth and say you don't know? Suppose your dinner is interrupted by a phone call solicitation. Do you act rudely or do you treat the person with respect? Suppose you notice that someone dropped some money from his or her purse or wallet while at the store. Do you pick it up and keep it, or do you return it to the person who dropped it?

You might think that returning lost change or talking politely with a telephone solicitor won't help you make hard ethical choices. What does your phone manner have to do with having an affair, cheating on taxes, or embezzling company funds? The truth is, if you're practiced at dealing with small ethical dilemmas, you'll be better able to tackle the really hard ones. If we are unethical in small issues and dilemmas, how can we think that we'll make good tough ethical decisions? The odds are high that if you are able to make good ethical decisions when it really counts, you probably also make good ethical decisions when there are only minor consequences and issues at stake.

So, the first step in making ethical decisions is to recognize that every decision is an opportunity to practice. How can you become more sensitive to these ethical issues? There's no simple formula for this, but there are some useful principles to follow. These issues will be covered in much more detail in chapter 2. For now, you need to get used to the question, "What are the ethical implications of my decision here?" If you can get used to the notion that every decision is a potential ethical decision, you'll likely be more open to see the range of ethical choices you have in front of you each and every day.

Step Two: What Are the Facts?

The next step is to gather your facts. What information do you need to obtain in order to make a good decision? You wouldn't buy a car unless you had conducted some research regarding the price, quality, style, and other factors that go into making such a decision. The same is true regarding ethical decision making. What facts must you get to make an informed decision? Who might you consult with to help guide you? What are the alternatives available to you?

Step Three: Examine the Alternatives

Third, you have to think through which ethical approach you plan on using when an issue hits you. You need to ask yourself if a common good, utilitarian, virtue, justice, or other approach is most appropriate in any given situation. You might consider examining your ethical dilemma through the lens of several different ethical approaches. For example, suppose you're trying to decide if you should cheat on your taxes. You may even try to justify your dishonest behavior by saying that you'll donate the savings to a charity. You may further justify your behavior by saying that you don't support the government's use of your tax dollars for military spending, polluting the environment, or paying handsome salaries to politicians. You might look at the utilitarian approach seeking to maximize the most happiness for the most people. It would make you and your family happy to keep the tax money, and the government might not even notice the money is missing. Then, you might consider using the absolute moral rule approach that might suggest that cheating and lying, no matter what the reason, is unethical. You might then choose to use a common goods approach to determine if cheating on taxes might harm the common good of society. The processes of looking at an ethical dilemma from different ethical points of view will likely help to fine-tune and deepen your thoughts regarding the issue. Hopefully, this will help you make the best decision.

Step Four: Make Your Decision

Next, make your decision and act on it. Once you have examined the various ethical approaches to the situation, you must make some decision. The decision may or may not be an easy one or a clear one. You may even decide to make what you consider an unethical decision because the price to pay for an ethical decision might be too high in your mind. For example, suppose you found a large sum of money in a wallet. You think about returning the money to the owner of the wallet because you generally support an absolute moral rule approach about honesty. However, you end up deciding to keep the money instead. You justify your decision because you are, perhaps, desperate for money and you will use it for a good cause, such as feeding your hungry children who might go without food otherwise. It's important to note that even if you decide to not behave in an ethical manner according to a particular ethical approach, you should think through the various ethical alternatives and understand the options that are available to you. In this way, you'll hopefully develop ethical problem-solving skills that can be used for future decisions.

Step Five: Consider Your Decision in Retrospect

Finally, evaluate your decision in retrospect. What did you decide to do and why? What do you think other reasonable people would have decided to do? After living with your decision for a while, would you make the same decision again? Looking at the consequences and outcomes of your decision will help you make better decisions in the future.

Conclusion

This chapter has highlighted nine different approaches to ethical decision making. These approaches have been used for hundreds if not thousands of years to help guide people in making good and ethical decisions. Being aware of them can help guide us today as we ponder our own ethical dilemmas. The five-step process for making ethical decisions gives you a framework for action. The next chapter highlights five ethical principles to live by and demonstrates how they can be used to help you make good daily ethical decisions.

Test Yourself

Take the three ethical approaches that were more relevant to you in this chapter, and use them to think through the following tough ethical dilemmas.

1. You discover that a good friend of yours is having an affair. You meet your friend's spouse whom you are also very close to. Do you tell him or her about your discovery of the affair? Why or why not?

2. You discover that your boss has been stealing large sums of money and supplies from work. Do you tell someone, or do you mind your own business? Why or why not?

3. You see someone with a gun running after another person on the street. It looks like the person with the gun is trying to kill the person he is chasing. You could trip or block the person with the gun as he or she runs by you. Do you? Why or why not?

CHAPTER 2

What Is Doing the Right Thing?

The last chapter focused on the various ways you can approach ethical questions and dilemmas. This chapter will introduce five ethical principles that you can use to guide your behavior and decision making in your personal and professional life (regardless of your line of work and living situation). These five principles can help you with both small and big ethical decisions. Subsequent chapters will look at each of the five principles in more detail.

The five basic ethical principles to live by are

> integrity

> competence

> responsibility

> respect

> concern.

While these five principles are certainly not cast in stone, they're a useful and productive way to think about how to live your everyday life. They can be applied to just about every ethical situation.

Where Do These Principles Come From?

These five principles didn't come out of thin air. They are, for example, in the code of ethics for psychologists developed and published by the American Psychological Association (APA 1992). However, they didn't originate there. These principles are distilled from several thousand years of moral philosophy, ethics, religious traditions, and so forth. For example, the Hippocratic oath was written about 2,500 years ago. While it was written for physicians of the time, the ethical principles it represents are relevant today.

The five principles can also be found in sacred scriptures from various religious traditions. Whether they come from the Hebrew Bible, the Christian New Testament, the Muslim Koran, or other sacred writings, integrity, competence, responsibility, respect, and concern for others are an important part of all these religious documents.

For example, treating others with respect is highlighted in many ancient scriptural texts. Here's a quote from the sacred Jewish Talmud: "Let the respect due to your companion be as precious to you as the respect due to yourself" (Mishna Avot 2:10). Concern and responsibility are emphasized in the Talmud and Hebrew Bible: "When the community is in trouble, a person should not say, 'I will go to my house and I will eat and drink, and my soul will be at peace.' A person must share in the concerns of the community as Moses did. Those who share in the community's troubles are worthy to see its consolation" (Babylonian Talmud, Ta'anit 11a). The importance of integrity is noted in many biblical passages, such as, "The Lord detests lying lips, but he delights in men who are truthful" (Proverbs 12:22). Justice and mercy are highlighted as well. For example, "And what does the Lord require of me, but to do justly, and to love mercy, and to walk humbly with my God?" (Micah 6:8).

Turning to the Christian New Testament, concern for others is a frequent theme in both the gospels as well as the writings of St. Paul. For example, in the Gospel of Matthew, it is reported that Jesus said: "Love your enemies and pray for those who persecute you" (Matthew 5:44). The chapter ends with Jesus saying, "Be compassionate, as your heavenly father is compassionate" (Matthew 5:44). Another example states that people should "... share with those in need" (Ephesians 4:28). Respect towards others is highlighted in many biblical references, such as, "Be devoted to one another in brotherly love. Honor one another above yourselves" (Romans 12:10).

All of the major religions of the world advocate integrity, responsibility, and concern and respect for others. Sadly, there are too many examples of people behaving, in the name of religion, in ways contrary to these ethical ideals. Many religious fundamentalists, regardless of religious tradition, have shown little respect for others who are different than them.

Why These Five Principles?

There are many potential ethical principles, phrases, and words that could be used rather than the five principles chosen to highlight in this book. These five were chosen because they are generally useful for most people, regardless of religious tradition, background, situation in life, or ethical perspective.

I also know from experience that these principles work. For many years, I have taught a seminar for psychology interns and postdoctoral fellows in child psychology and psychiatry at Stanford University Medical School. I also offer continuing education workshops on ethics for psychologists, social workers, psychiatric nurses, and marriage counselors. I've noticed over the years that these five principles not only work well in helping mental health professionals and trainees solve ethical dilemmas in their professional life, but they also help laypersons. In over twenty years of clinical practice, I've used these principles in helping clients solve ethical problems in their daily lives.

Why Not Use Other Ethical Principles?

You could use other ethical principles. There's nothing magical or perfect about these five. There are many others to choose from. For example, you could use the Ten Commandments from the Bible. Many people feel that following the Ten Commandments is a very useful and practical way to lead an ethical life regardless of your religious tradition. In fact, in recent years, many politicians across the United States have sought to have the Ten Commandments posted in all public schools. In fact, some politicians have gone so far as to say that if the Ten Commandments were posted in schools there would be less school-based violence and other problems (teen pregnancy, drug use). Whether you believe this bold assertion or not, it underscores the popularity of the Ten Commandments as a useful set of rules for living an ethical life.

You could use the list of traits promoted by the Boy Scouts of America (2002). The Boy Scouts believe in being

> trustworthy

> loyal

> helpful

> friendly

> courteous

> kind

> obedient

> cheerful

> thrifty

> brave

> clean

> reverent.

How would these traits work as a basis for living ethically? Most people would likely agree that being trustworthy, courteous, and kind are ethical principles worth following. However, some of these principles may be harder to follow or difficult to define or even support in certain circumstances. For example, being cheerful at a funeral might be inappropriate. Being thrifty might include being ungenerous with others.

The famous German theologian, Hans Kung has stated that all of the major world religions support six basic ethical principles of behavior (Kuschel and Haring 1993). These principles include avoiding killing, lying, stealing, and behaving immorally, while respecting parents and loving children. Again, like most of the principles already mentioned, most people would likely agree with these five tenets of behavior. Of course, some may be difficult to define and apply in all circumstances. For example, what is immoral in the view of some might be moral in the view of others. There may also be times when the ethical thing to do is to lie, steal, or kill. For example, killing a sniper who is in the process of killing a number of innocent victims might be the ethical thing to do in order to prevent additional deaths. Likewise, if telling the truth would result in the unjustifiable death of another person, then the ethical thing to do might be to lie.

In addition to many different lists of ethical principles to follow, there are vices that should be avoided in order to live an ethical life. For example, the famous writer, Dante Alighieri, as well as the famous theologian, Saint Thomas Aquinas, uses a well-known list of seven deadly sins:

> ‣ pride

> ‣ anger

> ‣ envy

> ‣ sloth

> ‣ avarice

> ‣ gluttony

> ‣ lust.

Then again, you may find it difficult to avoid these vices in everyday life. For example, does taking a vacation for a week count as being slothful? How much eating does it take to be considered gluttony? If you have a lustful or envious impulse but do not act upon it, is it still a sin or vice?

Thus, while there are many other possible lists of virtues or ethical principles to follow, the five principles mentioned earlier are relatively easy to use and remember and would be considered useful and productive by most people. Of course, you can use any list that you feel will benefit you.

In order to understand the five principles better, you need to know more about what is meant by each one and how to apply it to your life.

Understanding the Five Ethical Principles

What do we mean by *integrity, competence, responsibility, respect,* and *concern?* A brief definition, with some examples will be provided here. Some exercises follow to make these principles come to life for you.

Integrity

What do you think of when you think of the word *integrity?* I think of someone who is honest, fair, ethical, upright, moral, and a good person. What images come to your mind?

EXERCISE 2.1

What words or phrases come to your mind when you reflect on the word *integrity?* Write them down. Now, think of a person you know who has a great deal of integrity. What does this person do or say that makes you believe that he or she is indeed a person of integrity? What are the qualities or characteristics that you think best reflect integrity? Write them down here.

What has this brief exercise taught you about integrity? Do you admire these qualities that you noted? Do you consider yourself a person of integrity? Why or why not? In what ways do you maintain integrity and in what ways do you fail to do so? Be honest with yourself.

Having integrity means following high standards of honesty, justice, and fairness; the word *integrity* also means having completeness or wholeness. You could say that to maintain integrity means avoiding temptations or opportunities that would violate your completeness or wholeness.

Here's an example to illustrate this important ethical principle. If you had the chance to have highly pleasurable sex with a very attractive person without your spouse or committed partner ever knowing about the interaction, would you do it? Suppose you meet someone who's highly attractive to you while you're on a business trip or conference. Somehow you know that your spouse or committed partner will never learn about your liaison. Furthermore, you somehow also know that you would have no chance of contracting a sexually transmitted disease. You also suspect that the sexual encounter would be very pleasurable. In fact, you think it will be the most pleasurable sexual experience you've ever had in your life. Honestly, what do you think you would do? You could use the different ethical approaches discussed in chapter 1 to justify having or not having the sexual encounter. For example, the egoism or utilitarian approach might suggest that it's okay to have this sexual experience while the absolute moral rule and virtue approach might suggest that it's not okay to pursue this opportunity. If you were a person of integrity what would you do? You would likely decline the experience due to your vow of exclusive sexual activity with your spouse or committed partner.

This example demonstrates that integrity means behaving in a way that is consistent with your moral and ethical principles highlighting honesty, uprightness, and being beyond reproach.

Competence

What do you think of when you think of the word *competence?* I think of someone who is knowledgeable, skilled, knows his or her stuff, and is well trained, on top of his or her game.

EXERCISE 2.2

What words and phases come to your mind when you think of the word *competence?* Write them down. Think of a person you know who has a great deal of competence. What does he or she do or say that makes you believe he or she is so competent? Is this person competent in some areas and incompetent in other areas? If so, does he or she recognize these strengths and weaknesses? What kind of competencies do you have? What competencies do you wish you had? Write down your thoughts.

What has this brief exercise taught you about competence? What competencies do you most admire in yourself and others? Why? How are you competent? How are you incompetent? Again, try to be honest with yourself.

Competence means having the knowledge and skills that make you well qualified for a particular job or task. How do you know when you have enough competence? Let's face it, no one can be absolutely on the cutting edge of every issue in his or her field at all times. For example, an auto mechanic might not be able to keep up with all of the new aspects of automobiles for every make and model of car that he or she works on. A mechanic may continue training, but it might not be enough to maintain a high level of competence at all times. This incompetence could potentially result in a later traffic accident and death.

Even if you are fully competent at your job, there may be days or weeks that personal distractions, illness, mood, and so forth might get in the way of you performing at your highest level of competence. This is also true in personal matters. For example, you might be a competent parent but still have days when you are struggling to be a good enough parent. Perhaps you had a fight with your spouse or didn't get adequate sleep or felt highly distracted by something. During these times, your parenting skills may significantly suffer.

These issues highlight the complexity of obtaining and maintaining competence in your personal and professional life. Figuring out how to become and maintain competence in various aspects of your life is a highly challenging task. What criteria can you use to help guide you? These and other competence issues will be addressed in chapter 4.

Responsibility

What do you think of when you think of the word *responsibility?* The phrases that immediately come to my mind include "keeps promises," and "is aware of and attentive to obligations."

EXERCISE 2.3

Think of the word *responsibility*. What words and phases come to your mind? Write them down. Think of a person you know who is responsible. What does this person say that makes you feel that he or she is responsible? Is this person responsible in some areas and irresponsible in other areas? How are you responsible or irresponsible? Write down your thoughts.

What has this brief exercise taught you about being responsible? Be honest with yourself.

Being responsible means being accountable and following through on your obligations, promises, and commitments. Have you made promises that were never fulfilled? Of course, sometimes people forget their promises and thus their lack of follow-through is not intentional. However, sometimes people make promises they don't intend to keep, which can be disappointing and sometimes devastating for others.

Here is an example to illustrate the point. A psychotherapy client, Diane, is getting divorced. She states that while she loves her husband, he is so overcommitted to his work that he ignores his family responsibilities. He is never around, and she and their three children suffer for it. She sought a divorce because he did not live up to his promise to be an involved husband and father. Couples therapy and other interventions have failed to work.

Here's another example. There has been a great deal of attention in the media about Catholic priests who sexually abuse children. While any abuse of children is horrific, it is especially appalling when a clergy member perpetrates it. Research tells us that the percentage of Catholic clergy who sexually abuse children (about 2 and 5 percent) is consistent with male clergy from other religious traditions and is actually lower than the general population of males (Plante 1999, 2004). The outrage in the media and elsewhere over this problem is partly related to the lack of responsibility church officials exercised in preventing further abuse once they knew about it. Church officials have a responsibility to ensure that youth don't get abused by members of the clergy. Moving abusive clergy from parish to parish where additional abuse occurs is clearly irresponsible.

These examples focus on how individuals and groups have an obligation to behave in a responsible manner. Responsibility requires keeping promises and doing what you say you will do.

Respect

What do you think of when you think of the phrase, "respect for others' rights and dignity"? I think of someone who, treats others as he or she would want to be treated.

EXERCISE 2.4

Think of the word *respect*. What words and phases come to your mind? Write them down. Think of a person you know who is respectful of others. What does he or she do or say that makes you feel this way? Are he or she respectful in some areas and not in others? Write down your thoughts.

What has this brief exercise taught you about being respectful? How are you respectful to others? How are you disrespectful? Be honest with yourself.

Respect means treating others with attention, esteem, and consideration. Should you be respectful to people you do not like or with whom you disagree? For example, should you be respectful to neo-Nazis? Child molesters? Racists? These are difficult potential ethical conflicts. I will deal with them in more depth in subsequent chapters. However, for now, I'd suggest that all humans are worthy of respect as humans, regardless of their beliefs and behavior.

Concern

What do you think of when you think of the phrase "concern for others' welfare?" I think of someone who pays attention to and shows interest in the needs of others.

EXERCISE 2.5

Think of the phrase "concern for others." What words and phrases come to your mind? Write them down. Think of a person you know who is concerned about others. What does this person do or say that makes you feel that he or she is concerned about others? Does this person express concern for some people but not others? Is this person only concerned about his or her immediate family and friends? Is this person concerned about strangers? Write down your thoughts.

What has this brief exercise taught you about being concerned for others? How are you concerned for others? How are you unconcerned? Again, be honest with yourself.

What is our ethical responsibility to those who have less than we do? So many people around the world experience poverty, oppression, and natural disasters. Most of the six billion people on earth live without adequate food, clothing, shelter, or employment. Some people show their concern by donating money to worthy organizations that provide much needed services to others. Others work for non-profit agencies that help those in need. Other choose to do little, if anything, to help those in need.

It has been said that the best way to judge the commitment to ethics of any organization is to see how the management treats its lowest-paid members. What level of concern and interest should a company or organization show the lowest member of the organization? Unfortunately, there are no simple answers to such questions and dilemmas. We will discuss them in much more detail later on.

Cultivating the Five Ethical Principles

If you're hoping to filter your daily decisions through the lens of useful ethical principles, you'll need to find a way to easily remember the five ethical principles that you are using. One easy way to remember them is to use the acronym RRICC, which stands for *respect, responsibility, integrity, competence,* and *concern.* You can pronounce it like the male name "Rick."

Remember, the five ethical principles that are highlighted in this book are not cast in stone. You can choose to modify them or strive toward certain principles that are more meaningful to you. So, as you read this book and complete the various exercises, feel free to adapt the list so that the principles are tailored to your needs and values.

The next step is to seek good models of ethical behavior. You need to surround yourself with people who behave in an ethical way. Social psychology research over the course of many years has made it clear that people tend to model their beliefs and behavior after others. Parents see this principle in action when their child comes home from school with a new phrase, attitude, idea, perspective on events, and fashion sense. As adults, we also tend to compare our beliefs, attitudes, material possessions, parenting style, and so forth, with that of others. Therefore, the odds of making good ethical decisions in your daily life are low if you do not surround yourself with others of like mind.

You also need to reflect on your behavior and the behavior of others. You need to be able to evaluate and analyze decisions through the lens of ethics. At the beginning of the ethics seminar that I give for Stanford trainees, I ask them to start an ethics diary. They are asked to jot down each time they encounter an ethical dilemma and make a few notes about what the conflicting issues or ethical question is all about. During the beginning of the seminar, they have trouble coming up with many items between seminar sessions, but by the end of the seminar, they have numerous examples to share. Over time, if you practice, you too will be much more sensitive and attune to ethical issues. You will be better able to see subtle (and not so subtle) ethical dilemmas and be able to thoughtfully reflect on them.

You also need to test yourself. You need to have various experiences that help you understand what you are made of in terms of ethical behavior. You have likely heard the phrase, "It was a character-building experience." Adversity, challenges, troubles, and crises all provide tests of your character and your ethics. It is easy to feel that you are an ethical and moral person when everything goes your way and you have few troubles. It is very different if you have had challenging life experiences that have tested your character.

Finally, you need to find ways to repeatedly use these principles and learn from them. Again, if you can see ethical issues and act appropriately in your daily decisions, you'll be better able to make those really tough ethical decisions when you confront them.

Test Yourself

Use the RRICC model discussed in this chapter to think through these tough ethical dilemmas.

1. You have a sexually transmitted disease, such as herpes. You are dating someone you would very much like to have sex with. If your partner knew about your health condition, he or she might terminate the relationship. Do you tell him or her about your disease? Why or why not?

2. You're given a big raise at work because your boss believes that you made some excellent decisions that greatly helped the company. However, these decisions were not yours but came from another employee who no longer works there. Do you accept the raise? Do you tell anyone about where the decisions came from? Why or why not?

3. You are instructed to lay off 50 percent of the employees who report to you. One of the most competent members of your team is someone you don't get along with personally. Do you use this opportunity to lay off the person you dislike, which might be good for you but not in the best interest of the company? Why or why not?

PART 2

Five Ethical Principles to Guide All Decisions

CHAPTER 3

Integrity

The last chapter introduced five ethical principles that are easy to remember and use when dealing with everyday life as well as tough ethical decisions. This chapter will focus on the principle of integrity. It will highlight in more detail what integrity is and what it is not and then focus on how to build and develop integrity in both your work and personal life. Remember, integrity means following high standards of honesty, justice, and fairness and avoiding opportunities that would violate your completeness or wholeness.

EXERCISE 3.1

Think of someone who you believe is an excellent example of a person who maintains integrity. Is the person you are thinking about someone you know? Perhaps it is a famous person you have heard about in the news. What does this person do or say that makes you believe that he or she is a person of integrity? How would you define integrity when thinking of this person? Write it down.

What has this exercise taught you about integrity? What qualities do you think characterize people with integrity?

One person who many Americans think of as a person of integrity is former United States President Jimmy Carter. Unlike many other retired politicians who seem to spend their post-presidential years playing golf and giving expensive speeches, he's been very active in trying to help people throughout the developing world live in a more just way. For example, he's been very involved with helping countries conduct democratic, honest, and fair elections as well as helping poor countries improve their living conditions. He appears to be remarkably honest, which has at times, resulted in negative consequences for him. During his presidential campaign in 1976, he admitted in a *Playboy* interview (Sheer 1976) that he had lusted in his heart—an admission for which he was later ridiculed and scorned. While many might think of Jimmy Carter as being a man of integrity for his honesty, fairness, and commitment to justice, few Americans actually know him. Thus, most of us are unaware of what his motives and inner thoughts might be. Yet, many see him as someone who at least appears to be an excellent example of a person living with integrity.

The definition of integrity and above example suggest that someone with integrity follows a moral compass that isn't altered by temptations. Of course, no one is perfect, and even those who maintain a commitment to integrity can periodically make poor ethical decisions. The moral compass of a person of integrity might include a wide variety of qualities or characteristics. However, the three qualities that are perhaps the most productive to focus on are honesty, fairness, and justice. People with integrity value and uphold these important qualities.

Honesty

Honesty means telling the truth. However, for someone to maintain integrity, they need to be honest in a way that goes beyond just telling the truth. For example, people can be honest yet deceptive. How can this be?

Representing Your Credentials

A well-known author refers to himself as being "Harvard trained." He mentions this during his public lectures and it is written on the book jacket of his popular book. He did in fact receive some training at Harvard University, but his training consisted of a two-week summer workshop. His statement leads people to believe that he received his educational degree(s) there. While he is being honest (again, on the surface), his statement is deceptive.

You might ask, who cares? What's wrong with representing credentials in a deceptive manner? You might think that this has little if anything to do with making tough ethical decisions. An author might use the "Harvard trained" phrase to help sell books. No harm seems to be done with these deceptions. However, if someone has trouble being truly honest in small things, would you trust them to be honest in really difficult and challenging matters? How will people who are deceptive about rather small matters be about things that really count?

Honesty involves not only telling the truth but also behaving in a way to ensure that people aren't deceived or mislead by half-truths or omissions.

How honest should you be?

How far should you go to be honest? This is an important, complex, and difficult question to answer. You could argue that always telling the truth isn't always the most ethical thing to do.

Suppose, for example, you had a child you didn't want. Perhaps you got pregnant, considered having an abortion, and decided to have the baby anyway. Suppose the child grew up and asked you if he or she was wanted or unwanted. Would telling the truth needlessly hurt or harm the child? In this case, it might be more ethical to avoid the truth. So, what principles can help to guide you in determining your level of honesty?

When trying to decide if you should be honest, you might consider the various ethical approaches discussed in chapter 1. How would the utilitarian approach, the virtue approach, the egoism approach, and so on help to guide you? The utilitarian and egoism approach might suggest that you do not tell your child that he or she ws unwanted. The absolute moral rules approach might suggest that you do in fact tell the child the truth. Second, you could use the five-step ethical decision-making process that we discussed earlier to examine possible alternatives and options. For example, thinking through the various options and consequences of telling your unwanted child the truth might help you decide which approach to take. Finally, you could ask yourself if being honest is that important. If maintaining your integrity by being honest would result in your child getting very upset, then it might be more ethical to avoid the truth.

This example is a challenging one. It's not clear what the most ethical decision might be. Reasonable and ethical people could disagree about the best path to take. The desire to maintain integrity doesn't guarantee that the right decision will be made, but the effort at least helps to guide you in a manner that values honesty, fairness, and justice. These values can inform your decision making so that the probability of making a good ethical decision is high.

Informed Consent

Informed consent is an important concept in discussing honesty and integrity. Letting people know exactly what they're getting themselves into is what informed consent is all about. In this way, people can make decisions based on the best available information at the time. Take the example of the unwanted child. If a child is old enough to understand the meaning of consequences, you could try warning that such information might be hurtful to hear. Then you could let the child decide if he or she wants to hear the truth.

Fairness

"It's not fair!" You have surely heard this exclamation from an unhappy child or even an adult. Usually it means that someone is unhappy because they weren't treated in the same manner as someone else who was treated more favorably. People who have integrity treat others the way they would want to be treated. Of course, life isn't always fair. People are treated differently based on race, ethnicity, status, attractiveness, connections, money, and power. Many of the problems in our society are based on a lack of fairness.

Unfairness in Government

Many people complain that lobbyists have too much influence with elected officials. They argue that people who supply politicians with campaign donations and other gifts unfairly influence legislation that favors their companies and organizations. Arizona senator John McCain made campaign finance reform an issue in his 2000 presidential campaign. His argument was that donations and other favors from special interest groups have compromised the integrity of our political system and of individual congressmen and senators. His concern was that the latter do not pay enough attention to the average voter but favor those with power and money who can buy their way in.

Whom You Know

Another area where fairness is often discussed is in hiring. You would expect that the best-qualified applicant would get the job, regardless of who people are and whom they know. Of course, this is usually not the case. In fact, most people secure their jobs through connections. If you have better connections, you get better jobs. Is this fair?

Misleading Others

People often use deception to get an unfair advantage. For example, Beth proudly talked about how she secured a table at a busy and popular restaurant when she didn't have a reservation. Her strategy was to behave towards the restaurant hostess as if she did in fact have a reservation. She lied by stating that her secretary had made reservations for her, and she acted as if the restaurant had made an error. Since the hostess could not find the reservation and believed Beth's claim, she also assumed that someone at the restaurant had made an error. The hostess hastily sought to accommodate Beth as well as provide a free glass of champagne to compensate for the "mix up."

Beth didn't treat the restaurant or the other patrons in a fair manner. In order to accommodate Beth, others probably had to wait longer for their table or were turned away. Perhaps the host or hostess making reservations got in trouble. Again, a little white lie can have rather serious unforeseen consequences. Furthermore, what are the odds that Beth would tell the truth about a really tough ethical dilemma if she easily lied in order to eat at the restaurant without a reservation?

Someone who maintains integrity strives to be fair in his or her interactions and decisions. This, of course, is not always easy. For example, suppose your spouse accidentally hurts or even kills someone while driving a car. Your spouse had been drinking alcohol, and new anti-drunk driving laws in your state mean that he or she might have to serve a significant time in jail. Other people who committed a similar offence have served or are serving a strict jail sentence. Fairness would suggest that your spouse receive the punishment that others have also received. Do you try to use your influence, money, or power to secure a more lenient sentence for your spouse? Suppose you are wealthy, well connected with the legal profession, or have other advantages that others don't have. Of course, you would likely be motivated to do whatever you could to help your spouse cope with the situation.

A person of integrity tries to be fair to all. The rules apply to everyone, regardless of who they are and whom they know. How far will you go to be fair?

Justice

While honesty, fairness, integrity, and justice overlap to some degree in terms of definition, it's important to discuss the meaning of each to give you a fuller picture of what integrity means. Justice certainly involves both fairness and honesty, but seeking justice seems to go beyond honesty and fairness. It also refers to making things right by trying to correct current and past wrongs.

Delayed Justice

Recently, a man in his seventies was convicted of a church bombing that he apparently participated in about forty years ago during racial tensions in Alabama. Several African-American children were killed and others were severely injured. The man has not experienced any trouble with the law since, and doesn't appear to be a threat to others now. His jail sentence is about justice, however, not about protecting the public from a violent person who might harm future potential victims. After his recent trial and conviction, many surviving victims and their families reported feeling that "justice was served." They were referring to the fact that, although it took many years to try and convict the man, he was finally held accountable for his crimes.

The elderly and infirm former Chilean president Augusto Pinochet was tried in England for crimes against humanity that occurred during his administration decades earlier. Elderly Nazi war criminals have been captured tried, convicted, and even executed many years after World War II. In these cases, these men didn't pose a current or future threat to society. Therefore, putting them in jail didn't make society a safer place. Their conviction and jail sentence was all about justice.

While seeking justice certainly doesn't negate wrongdoing, bring back to life the killed person, or take away the trauma that victims and their families experienced, it does seek to make people accountable for their behavior and attempt to righten, as best as possible, a wrong.

How is justice served in your everyday life? How does a person of integrity seek justice in his or her day-to-day decisions?

Justice in the Workplace

Suppose you find out that some people in your company are not receiving a living wage. Their salaries are too small to support themselves in the community. Many entry-level employees as well as employees who make minimum wage (custodial staff, day care workers, fast food workers) have great difficulty earning enough money for basic needs such as food and housing. News reports frequently mention that some full-time employees are homeless. Justice would seek to ensure that everyone who works should earn enough money to support his or her basic needs. This seems especially crucial in companies where large profits are made and some employees make much more than a living wage. How can a company justify paying high-level executives millions of dollars in salary and bonuses and perhaps sponsor lavish parties and events for top executives when they don't pay their custodial staff a living wage? How could a full-time employee at a company be homeless when top executives live lavishly?

A person of integrity might talk with various people in the company about living wage concerns, making it clear that it's unjust that some employees aren't receiving an adequate living wage. He or she might point out that the situation is not fair when others in the company are making a great deal of money, well beyond what they need to live comfortably. Seeking justice might suggest that more action is needed. A person of integrity might argue that the living wage issue is a matter of justice and that a just response by the company would be to increase these low wages. Perhaps the fairly easy and low-cost ethical decision for you in this situation would be to take your concern to appropriate persons in the company. The tougher ethical dilemma is to decide if you want to work for a company or organization that does not provide a living wage for all its employees. Would you consider quitting your job over this issue?

These examples highlight the notion that justice goes beyond fairness and honesty. It seeks action to correct a wrong.

How Do You Build Integrity?

How can you strive towards being a person of integrity? How do you instill this characteristic in your children? How can you maintain integrity when tempted to do otherwise? There are no easy or simple answers. However, there are some principles that can guide you in your efforts.

You Need to Want It

Do you want to be a person of integrity? On the surface, perhaps almost everyone would say yes. Who would say no? Yet, being a person of integrity might mean that you have to bypass certain advantages or perks. It's easy to maintain integrity when there are no significant costs to you. It's much harder to be honest, fair, and just when there may be negative consequences around the corner. If you didn't care about honesty, fairness, justice, and maintaining a moral compass, you might be better able to gain wealth, power, and influence. Somehow, you must need to feel secure in the desire to maintain integrity, even when it will cost you. This is where those tough ethical dilemmas come into focus.

EXERCISE 3.2

Take a moment to examine why you want to be a person of integrity. Close your eyes for a minute and think about why you want to strive towards honesty, fairness, and justice. What do you come up with? Write down your thoughts.

What will motivate you to seek integrity? What must you do or experience to help you develop this desire? Sometimes seeing a model (someone else behaving with integrity) can help you. Sometimes having traumatic experiences where you come to an ethical crossroads can help you better seek integrity. Do you want to be a person of integrity? Why or why not?

You Must See It Everywhere

You need to see almost all decisions as decisions involving integrity. Big or small, just about all decisions and interactions can test your integrity.

I remember replacing the windows in my home a number of years ago. After researching the different types and styles of windows available on the market, I was much more attentive to windows wherever I went. The same was true when I bought a car. Again, after researching information about cars, I noticed the year, make, model, and style of every car on the road. The same is true for integrity. If you sensitize yourself to issues of integrity, you'll see them everywhere. If you see that decisions and interactions are opportunities to act with integrity, you'll see these opportunities more clearly and more often.

You may recall the Columbine High School murders that occurred in April 2000. A survivor apparently overheard one of the two gunman ask a girl if she believed in God. The girl replied, "yes" and then was immediately shot to death. Let's look at this horrific scene a bit more closely.

The two angry boys were intent on killing as many students and teachers as possible before killing themselves. Before shooting her, they asked the girl if she believed in God. Of course, we don't know what the boys would have done if she answered, no. Some news reports stated that the boys denied a belief in God and were perhaps angry at church institutions, organized religion, and God. We don't know exactly what was going on in the mind of these boys or their victims. Did the girl know that she would die if she answered yes? Did she think she would have been spared if she answered, no? It appears that she answered the question with honesty (and integrity), and the consequences were deadly.

Many others throughout history have died for their beliefs and values. Sadly and tragically, people of all faiths have died because of their beliefs and identification with a particular religious tradition. For example, Jews who did not hide their Jewishness during the Holocaust faced certain death. Tragically, this has been true for various Jewish groups throughout history. Many early Christians were also executed for their beliefs. Many Muslims were killed during the Inquisition when they refused to convert to Christianity. These victims were acting with integrity even though their beliefs and identity resulted in death.

This is perhaps one of the most difficult ethical decisions you can make. Would you die for your ethical principles?

EXERCISE 3.3

How far would you go to maintain integrity and a sense of honesty? Would you die being honest rather than being spared for lying? Would you have tried to hide (or lie about) your identity in the Holocaust if you would be spared? Frankly, I think that I would indeed do what I could (even if it involved lying) in order to survive, as long as no one else would get killed as a result of my deceit. What about you? Imagine you're being persecuted for your belief or identity. Suppose you were Jewish and hiding in Europe during the Holocaust, the Crusades, or the Inquisition. Suppose someone asked you if you believed in God, and you knew that a truthful response would result in your death. What would you say? Close your eyes and visualize these scenes.

What have you learned about yourself in this exercise? How far will your desire for integrity and honesty take you? What are the limits of your striving towards these goals?

EXERCISE 3.4

Here's another exercise to help fine-tune your thinking about applying the principle of integrity to your life. Think of all of the decisions and interactions you've had during the past twenty-four hours. Can you recall experiences and opportunities where you behaved with or without integrity? Review your appointment book. How did you behave with (or without) integrity during the past day?

What have you learned from this exercise? Perhaps you didn't notice any opportunities for behaving with integrity. Perhaps you noticed a lot. During the next twenty-four hours, try to ask yourself if each experience, interaction, and decision is one that provides you with an opportunity to behave with integrity or not.

Model It

One way to increase the chances that you'll act with integrity is to surround yourself with people who are also striving towards this same goal. This has several important advantages. First, you can observe behaviors and decisions that show integrity in others. You can model your own behavior after those who make good decisions in similar circumstances. Second, you can model integrity for others. Your children, peers, coworkers, and employees likely learn more from what you do than what you say. While it's easy to tell others to be honest and fair, it's harder to model these behaviors for them. Third, social support from like-minded people is very powerful. Social psychologists have demonstrated in a variety of ways that people constantly compare themselves to others and adjust their behavior based on social norms. Surrounding yourself with people of integrity provides you with social support, encouragement, and social reinforcement to be a person of integrity yourself.

Having an ethical model can help you strive towards good ethical decisions. Who do you admire as an ethical model in your life? If you don't have an ethical model, can you get one?

EXERCISE 3.5

Who are the models of integrity in your life? Who can you model yourself after? Make a list. Does their behavior help to inspire you to act better? Do certain people represent particular behaviors that you find inspiring? What are the behaviors?

What has this exercise taught you? Do you have a model? If not, why not? If you do, how do they guide or inspire you to behave in an ethical manner?

Test It

To build integrity, you must be tested. While it's easy to say that you are honest, fair, just, and a person of integrity, it's quite another thing to behave in this way all the time and to experience negative consequences that behaving with integrity might involve. This is where some tough ethical decisions arise.

For example, suppose you're trying to be more honest in your interactions with others. You're attempting to make a sale and you're being as honest as possible about the pros and cons of the product or service you're selling. Will your sales figures go up or down if you're totally honest? Will you lose your job if you don't meet these important sales goals? Will losing you're job or not making your sales goals hurt your family's well being?

Here's another example to consider. You're looking for a new job. Suppose you're out of work and you're worried about making ends meet. Perhaps you have a family to support as well. You are interviewed for a position and you suspect that being completely honest during the interview may result in your not getting the job. What would you do?

How can you be tested? Think of some examples during recent weeks when you may not have handled a situation with honesty. What would happen if you could relive the experience but this time be fully honest? What would the consequences be?

It has been said that challenging life experiences build character. The stress of abuse, poverty, being a victim of crime, serious illness, divorce, death of loved ones, and other difficult life events have a way of shaping you into a certain type of person. The famous philosopher Fredrich Nietzsche once said: "That which does not kill us makes us stronger."

EXERCISE 3.6

How have you been tested in life? Write down the ten worst things that have happened to you. Number them from one to ten. Next to each one, write down how the experience changed you. How has each experience changed you for the better or for the worse? Now, write down how these experiences challenged your integrity. Some may have challenged your integrity, while some may not have. That's okay. Have these experiences increased your integrity? Why or why not?

Challenging life experiences have a way of grounding you. These experiences test and help develop your character.

What has this exercise taught you? Have your life challenges helped to make you a person of integrity? Why or why not?

Coping with Mistakes

No one's perfect. Everyone makes errors. Everyone gives into temptations sometimes. Those who wish to maintain the highest levels of integrity in their daily lives are likely to behave without integrity now and then. So, how do you cope with these lapses? How do you get back on the horse when you've fallen off?

Any behavior is hard to change or maintain. For example, the vast majority of people who try to lose weight regain their weight loss within a few years. In fact, research from the University of Pennsylvania found that over 90 percent of people who lost weight regained all of their weight within five years (Wadden et al. 1989). Most people who quit drinking alcohol drink again at some point. The best intentions don't necessarily result in perfect behavior forever.

A woman named Lynn said that when she was a young child, she stole candy from a local market. She was so overwhelmed by guilt that, for several years, she would throw money on the floor of the store in order to make up for her ethical or moral lapse. While throwing money on the floor of the market didn't negate her earlier stealing, it was a way for a young child to compensate for her error or lapse in judgment.

How do you react when you chose to not behave in an ethical manner? How do you recover from an ethical lapse in integrity?

If you fall short of your goal to behave with integrity at all times, do not give up. You need to develop strategies to deal with your lapses and try to maintain integrity in the future. You can recognize an ethical lapse and try to recover from it by changing your future behavior.

EXERCISE 3.7

Think of a time when you didn't behave with integrity. Perhaps you were dishonest or unfair to someone. What might you do or say differently to avoid this error in the future? How might you try to correct the wrong, if possible?

Conclusion

Integrity is the foundation for living an ethical life. It involves being honest, fair, just, whole, and following a moral compass. This moral compass is challenged each day with temptations to behave in an unethical manner. We are often tempted to behave in a dishonest and unfair manner to obtain short-term gains. Although the best intentions may still result in poor decisions, if you're committed and highly motivated to maintain integrity, as well as model it for others and seek models for yourself, you will be more likely to make good ethical decisions that maintain integrity. Furthermore, if you surround yourself with people of like mind, have coping strategies for dealing with lapses, and are sensitive in seeing integrity issues everywhere, you'll increase your chances of developing ethical muscle. If you can maintain your integrity regarding small matters and get into the habit of behaving with integrity in your daily life, then you'll be more likely to act with integrity when the really tough issues and dilemmas come your way.

Test Yourself

Use what you have learned to make tough ethical decisions.

1. You find out that your child was drunk and involved in a hit-and-run accident that severely hurt someone. Do you go to the police? Why or why not?

2. You find a suitcase with a million dollars in cash in it. Do you keep it? Why or why not?

3. The contractor who is building your home has made an accounting error and undercharged you $10,000 for the work conducted on the house. Do you correct the error?

CHAPTER 4

Competence

The last chapter covered integrity, which is essential to living an ethical life. Without integrity, it would be impossible to develop and nurture most other ethical qualities. In this chapter, the focus will be on competence. We must be competent in our personal and professional lives in order to live an ethical life and do the right thing. How can we be ethical if we're incompetent in our various roles and duties in life? Like all ethical principles, being competent is easier said than done. How do you know exactly what competence is and is not? How can you tell if you're competent enough in your various roles? What can you do to maintain competence? What do you do if you find yourself to be incompetent in certain areas of your life or at certain times? How can you motivate yourself to strive toward competence? These are some of the challenging question to address in this chapter.

What does competence have to do with ethics? If you say that you're a car mechanic, people expect that you know how to evaluate and repair problems with cars that you specialize in working with (such as Hondas or Fords). If you say you're a friend, then people will expect you to be friendly with them and show concern for them. Competence is related to integrity in that maintaining your roles in life assumes that you're competent in those roles. You would not be behaving with integrity if you said that you were a competent piano teacher, for example, but were unable to competently teach piano. So, in order to behave ethically, you must be able to achieve and maintain competence in the areas that you claim you are competent in.

Competence means being good enough at your job, as well as being good enough as a parent, driver, friend, lover, citizen, and so forth. What is good enough, and how do you evaluate your competence?

EXERCISE 4.1

Think about the different roles that you have in your life. Think about your role at your job. Think about the other roles you might have as a mother, father, friend, driver, or citizen. List the five most important roles you have. Write them down in order of importance to you. Next, ask yourself if you are competent in each of those roles. You may have days when you feel more competent in a particular role relative to other days. That's understandable. Try to think of your average level of competence in each of your five major roles. You may want to rate yourself on a scale of 1 to 10, where 1 is completely incompetent and 10 is fully competent. Score yourself in each of the five categories. Now, rate yourself again using the same scale, based on your perception of how others who know you best in each role would judge you. For example, how would other drivers or people who drive with you rate you as a driver? How would your boss and coworkers rate your competence at work? How would your spouse and children rate you as a parent? Perhaps you could ask them to rate you as well.

What have you learned about yourself in this exercise? Are you highly competent in all that you do? Do others think of you as highly competent? Are you competent in some areas but not in others? What are the consequences of not being competent in one or more of your roles?

How Do You Know If You Are Competent?

The trouble with this self-assessment exercise is that it's often very difficult if not impossible for us to adequately judge our level of competence in most areas of life. Research has indicated that incompetent people generally have no idea that they're incompetent (Kruger and Dunning 1999). Most people tend to see themselves in a favorable light. Of course, people who are depressed or who experience low self-esteem tend to reflect on their competencies in a very negative manner. Curiously, research has found that people who are depressed tend to be more realistic than nondepressed people when evaluating their own competence, and that most people overestimate their skills and competencies.

Here's and example, involving how people drive and how they perceive themselves behind the wheel. Some people who are generally good drivers make errors that, in the moment, make them incompetent. For example, suppose someone cuts you off on the freeway by switching lanes too abruptly. What would you think about that person? Would you think that the other driver is competent? Probably not. Now, suppose *you* were the person who cut someone off. Would you think you were an idiot? Would you think you were an incompetent driver? Probably not. You would likely use some excuse to explain your driving error, such as, "I was distracted by something."

You might wonder, what does this have to do with ethics? Every time you drive, you are putting yourself and others at some risk of injury and death. Traffic accidents do happen, and most are caused by distraction, alcohol or other substance abuse and misuse, and other human errors. If you drive after drinking too much alcohol or if you drive knowing that your brakes aren't working properly, or if you drive when you are very upset, then you are likely to be an incompetent driver. Being incompetent behind the wheel of a car or other motor vehicle will greatly increase your chances of being in an accident. You could argue that being incompetent behind the wheel is unethical.

Avoiding Double Standards

The above driving situation illustrates how we tend to see others in *dispositional* terms, meaning we attribute a chronic and enduring dispositional characteristic to explain the behaviors of others. For example, "He went through the red light because he's an idiot," or, "She cut me off because she's an aggressive driver." However, we tend to experience our own behavior (especially when it's bad) in *situational* terms. For example, "I went through the red light because I misjudged how fast I was going," or, "I cut that person off on the freeway because of a blind spot."

These important distinctions can help you better understand how you evaluate competence in yourself and in others. When it comes to evaluating competence, you probably tend to see others in black-and-white dispositional terms. For example, you might say, "My boss is an idiot and is so clueless," or you might say that your doctor is "fabulous." People tend to believe that others are either competent or incompetent and that it is a dispositional quality that is enduring.

Meanwhile, we tend to overestimate our own level of competence and evaluate any negative or problematic behavior in ourselves in more situational terms (Kruger and Dunning 1999). For example, following criticism in a work performance review, you might say that you would be better at your job if you got more training or useful feedback. You might say that it isn't your fault but the fault of management, too high expectations, not enough resources, poor quality coworkers, and so forth. If you received negative feedback from a boss or coworker, you might get defensive, blaming something or someone other than yourself. You also might blame the messenger. One of the reasons why most people don't want to deliver bad news to others (especially when it involves corrective feedback) is because they're likely to get blamed (and perhaps victimized) by the person receiving the feedback.

Thus, it's common to experience a bias when evaluating your own competencies. Most people don't get up in the morning thinking they're incompetent in the various roles that they have at work and at home. Unless the incompetence is blatant or the consequences are severe, we tend to go about our business assuming that we're competent in all that we do.

Assessing Your Competencies

There are certain roles that we play that make it very clear if we are competent or not. It's hard not to notice incompetence in professional sports, for example. If you're an incompetent batter, in baseball, then you won't get hits and your batting average will be very low. If you're an incompetent fielder, then you'll make many errors. You certainly won't last long in professional baseball if you're incompetent in batting or fielding. Most roles in life aren't so clear-cut. While certain behaviors might be clearly competent or incompetent behaviors in any of these roles, many behaviors might not be so clear.

So, how can you tell if you're competent or not in what you do? It depends on what role you are playing and what criteria can be used to examine your competence. However, there are some useful principles or guidelines that can help you better understand if you're competent or not.

Seeking Objective Criteria

Earlier, you listed the five most important roles or positions you have in life. Look at the list again and ask yourself if there are any objective criteria that can help you evaluate your level of competence in each of those five roles.

If you're a parent, what determines your level of competence? The actress Roseanne Barr said, "I figure if my kids are alive at the end of the day, I've done my job." She suggested humorously that her criterion for competent parenting is relatively low. While you may have days when you feel that way, you probably think that more is necessary to be considered a competent parent.

You could come up with an objective list of what you might consider competent parenting. Your list might include ensuring that children are adequately feed, clothed, sheltered, and nurtured, and are not neglected or abused. Yet it's not always obvious what the criteria would be for each of these categories. Furthermore, there may be certain exceptions to these guidelines. For example, someone who is very poor but is a competent parent might have trouble feeding, clothing, and sheltering their child. On the other hand, a wealthy person who has no trouble providing the basic necessities might be emotionally neglectful or physically abusive.

EXERCISE 4.2

Try this exercise to make the competencies in your life more concrete. Look over your list of the five roles you play, and ask yourself if there are objective criteria that you can use to evaluate your level of competence in these five roles. Write down what the criteria would be for each role.

What have you learned from this exercise? Are there clear criteria that you can use to evaluate your competencies? If not, how might you figure out how to evaluate yourself?

Getting Feedback

Next you should try to get effective, unbiased, and useful feedback about your competence in these areas. It's not always easy to get effective feedback from others, however. Many people may not want to hurt your feelings and thus they may not state what they honestly feel about your performance. Others might have a hidden agenda and as a result might be motivated to evaluate you in a particularly positive or negative light. Others might not really know what you do or how you perform because they don't watch you very closely. Therefore, you need to try to get objective feedback knowing that there may be significant limitations.

EXERCISE 4.3

Next to your list of five roles, make a list of people in your life who can be good judges of your competence in each role. Who can best judge your level of competence at work, at home, and so forth? Write down their names. If you haven't already done so, can you ask each person that you listed to give you an honest evaluation of your competence in the role that they know you best? Can you ask them to evaluate your strengths and weaknesses in this role?

What has this exercise taught you? Can you find enough people who can give you objective and thoughtful feedback? What can you learn from them?

Avoiding Defensiveness

Getting feedback isn't always easy. Criticism is often very difficult to hear. Most people usually respond to criticism with defensiveness, excuses, denial, rationalization, and other strategies to dismiss the negative feedback. Sometimes there are good reasons to get defensive. Sometimes feedback isn't on target. Sometimes feedback is meant to hurt you rather than to help you. But if feedback is well-intentioned and you're truly open to an objective and thoughtful evaluation of your competencies, then you can better avoid defensiveness. Again, this is easier to say than to do.

How can you avoid being defensive? There are a few fairly simple principles that can guide you. For starters, you should write down the feedback so that you can look it over later, avoiding the initial emotional response that you may have the moment you hear something that's critical. Second, you shouldn't say anything about the feedback when it's delivered to you but only listen and write it down carefully. Third, you might consider asking another appropriate and knowledgeable person to review the feedback and determine what appears reasonable and what might be unreasonable.

Suppose you go through the process of looking at the objective criteria for evaluating your level of competence, getting effective feedback, and avoiding defensiveness. You then find out that you aren't adequately competent in one of your roles. What can you do to best deal with your own incompetence in an ethical manner? Of course, what you will do will depend on the role in question.

Hector's Story

A man named Hector told a remarkable story about his experience as a father when his son Mike was a very young infant. Mike had a very high fever. Hector called his pediatrician, and the advice nurse told him to bring Mike to the local emergency room. An emergency physician resident, (a newly graduated doctor) who was just beginning her residency training, was assigned to evaluate Mike. The physician had started her position just six weeks earlier. She determined that she needed to conduct several invasive tests, including a spinal tap. A spinal tap involves delicately inserting a needle into the spinal cord area to obtain cerebral spinal fluid. She had never performed a spinal tap on such a young child before. The attending physician supervising the young resident also had little experience performing this medical procedure on such a young child. After the doctors made several failed attempts, the hysterical parents refused to allow them to continue this trial-and-error method with their infant son. Eventually, the doctors determined that Mike had a urinary tract infection, and he was given high doses of antibiotics, which ultimately fixed the problem.

Medical training programs throw doctors into a system and experience that they aren't usually prepared for. The doctors have to sink or swim. While it may not be the doctor's fault that she was placed in a situation where she was incompetent, she should have dealt with her incompetence in an ethical manner. How might this happen? She might get appropriate consultation (from the attending physician or a pediatrician on call) as soon as possible. She might only do a procedure that she feels that she can adequately conduct. She might be honest with the parents and not fake skills that she doesn't have already.

Sometimes you're thrown into situations where you're incompetent and yet must act. How you handle these situations becomes the ethical challenge. When faced with your own incompetence, how do you ethically respond if you are forced to act in some way that challenges your abilities?

How Do You Obtain Competence?

Once you realize that you're incompetent or lack competence in a certain area, you can develop a plan to achieve competence.

In the example above, the young doctor could seek out appropriate consultation and information to reach competence as soon as possible. She could be honest with her patients and colleagues as well. However, it's important to note that she could potentially lose her job or create chaos for the hospital if she were to behave ethically. It may be that the hospital staff or others would expect her to be less frank about her limitations. She might be faced with the tough decision of either acting ethically or severely damaging her career. For example, her boss might tell her not to fully inform her patients that she is inexperienced or unable to competently perform a particular procedure. What do you think she should do under those circumstances?

What about you? In what areas, if any, of your life are you incompetent? In what areas of your life do you seek more competence? Your strategies to obtain competence will vary depending upon the area you are concerned about. For example, your efforts to be a more competent worker will be very different from your efforts to be a more competent friend. However, there are several useful general principles that can guide you.

Desire It

You can't improve your competence in an area unless you want to do it. Are you willing to do what it takes to improve your competence? While this might seem to be an obvious question, it's important to ask yourself how important it is to you to improve your competence in a particular area.

EXERCISE 4.4

Here's an exercise to determine your level of commitment. Make a list of the areas in your life that you'd like to be more competent in. Write them down. Then, organize your list, ranking highest the areas that you most desire to be competent. Now, rate your desire for competence on a scale of 1 to 10, in which 1 reflects no motivation and 10 reflects extremely high motivation. Use the scale to evaluate your level of motivation to achieve competence in each area.

What have you learned from this exercise? Are you highly motivated to develop competencies in some areas but not others? In order to have a reasonable chance of changing behavior and developing new and improved competencies, you need to want it.

Find a Role Model

Can you find a model of competence that you can learn from? Perhaps you know or can observe someone who is an expert in the area where you most want to improve your competence. Having a mentor or consultant can help you to develop the necessary skills. For example, many schools assign new teachers to an experienced, senior teacher. The new teacher might observe the more experienced teacher in class and regularly consult with the senior colleague. You can do the same in the area where you want to achieve more competence.

Make a Roadmap

Once you have both a desire and a model for competence, you'll need to have a roadmap or plan that reflects your efforts to achieve your goal. Your plan will obviously be based on what you're trying to achieve. However, you should develop a written plan that is based on realistic chunks of progress. Does your competence plan mean reading books, getting training, going back to school, or being mentored by someone? The plan should be specific and as detailed as you can make it. You'll also want to include timelines and both short- and long-term goals. Are there objective criteria that you could use to determine exactly what you're trying to achieve? Perhaps you could detail specific criteria that would help you to determine if you've reached competence.

Suppose, for example, you would like to be more competent as a parent. What kind of plan would you develop? You might want to spend some time taking parenting classes or reading parenting books. You might want to observe excellent and competent parents in action. This could be done in a formal way (an organized parent training or mentoring program) or an informal way, by watching people parent in public. You might want to ask others whom you trust to evaluate your parenting skills by offering feedback and suggestions based on their observations. You might want to start with a specific behavior or parenting dilemma. For example, perhaps you'd like to work on getting your children to clean up their rooms without yelling at them. Perhaps you'd like to work on getting your children to eat dinner at the kitchen table without the television on. Maybe you'd like to work on getting the children up in the morning in a timely manner so that they'll not be late for school.

EXERCISE 4.5

Take the list that you developed in the last exercise, outlining areas in which you'd like to be more competent. After each item on your list, create a plan to accomplish your goal. Include a time frame to evaluate your progress. What do you hope to achieve in one month? Six months? A year? Include people who can act as mentors, model, or consultants. Include specific behaviors that you would like to acquire.

What have you learned from this exercise? Are your goals realistic? Are your plans realistic? Can you identify consultants or models? Why or why not?

How Do You Maintain Competence?

Once you achieve competence, then what? How do you maintain the competencies that you acquire once they're established? In many areas, today's competent behavior is tomorrow's incompetent behavior. For example, suppose you're really good at being a medical doctor. Perhaps you have a real talent for it. Due to technological and scientific advances in recent years, however, many of your skills and techniques may have become obsolete. Good clinical medical skills are transferable, but there are many aspects of modern medicine that don't involve the skills you developed in the past. Just because you were a fabulous doctor many years ago doesn't mean that you'll be a fabulous doctor today. This raises a very important ethical issue, because as a doctor your competence or lack thereof could mean the difference between life and death. In many areas, competencies atrophy very quickly unless they are nurtured by constant training and experience.

So, how do you maintain competence? The principles discussed earlier in this chapter can help you here as well.

Find Motivation

First, you need to want to maintain competence and do the necessary work to ensure that you retain your competence. You may have developed a variety of skills and competencies over the years. As time goes by, however, you may need to choose which ones you will maintain and which ones you will allow to atrophy.

In which areas of your life do you most want to maintain your competency? Are you willing to let some of your skills atrophy?

Seek Mentors and Models

Second, you need to ensure that you have adequate models, consultants, mentors, and so forth so that you can best observe what competence looks like in others. It's difficult to maintain competence in many areas unless you're able to observe it in others. For example, reading about surgical procedures and techniques in a textbook or medical journal might not help a doctor maintain competence as much as observing highly competent models in an operating room. If you want to maintain your competence speaking a foreign language, you'll likely need to do more than read books written in the language of interest. You'll likely need to observe others speak and allow yourself to converse with others in the language as well.

Develop a Game Plan

In order to maintain competence you need to develop a game plan as to how you'll work towards achieving competence at all times. Some ideas are taking refresher classes, meeting regularly with a model or consultant, taking continuing education workshops, reading up-to-date information on the topic of interest, and getting regular corrective feedback. All of the above will help you keep your level of competence high.

Letting Go

Perhaps one of the more difficult aspects of maintaining competence is realizing that there are some areas in your life that you just cannot keep up with and thus you will need to let those competencies go. This is difficult because it means asking yourself to objectively evaluate your skills and to acknowledge that you are no longer competent in an area that you once were highly competent in.

EXERCISE 4.6

Review your list of competencies from exercise 4.1. Which ones should you let go of? Which ones should you maintain? What plan do you have to maintain competencies? Who can help you achieve your goals?

How Do You Deal with Lapses?

How do you deal with lapses, when you fall into incompetent behavior? What should you do when you are confronted with a moment of potential incompetence?

This is where the ethical foundation of integrity discussed in the previous chapter can help. You need to first tap into your sense of integrity to find a way of dealing with the inevitable circumstances where you fall into incompetence. For example, suppose you are a teacher who has been teaching first grade for many years but are now asked to teach sixth grade instead. Suppose you are a lawyer who specializes in tax law but you want to practice criminal law.

A teacher might want to observe and consult with colleagues about the new class assignment. A lawyer might also observe and consult with another lawyer or perhaps participate in additional training. Generally, it's important to approach these situations with integrity. That is, be honest, fair, just, and forthright. You might be truthful with others about your limitations. In this way, you are giving people informed consent. You are letting them know what your strengths and weaknesses are and what you're trying to do to achieve competence.

Maintaining integrity when dealing with your competencies or lack of competencies also means being truthful and honest with yourself. It's very hard to conduct a self-appraisal that might result in the realization that you're no longer competent in an important area.

Jean's Story

Jean is a woman who has been having severe troubles with alcohol and other substance abuse and addiction problems. She has three small children and is trained as a nurse. She knows that her competencies as a nurse and parent have significantly declined in recent months. She has been having a great deal of trouble being a good enough nurse and parent. She admits that she needs to rely on her competent coworkers and husband to do the majority of her duties. She also admits that she needs to better manage her substance abuse problem and resulting depression before she can be a competent nurse and parent once again. Although it's painful for her to admit that she no longer feels like a competent nurse and parent, she has the integrity to be honest with herself, to acknowledge her weaknesses and limitations, and make appropriate plans for the welfare of her patients and children.

Once you're honest with yourself and others, you're then ready to develop a specific coping plan to deal with your lapse. This might involve seeking consultation, training, reading, and so on. It might involve apologizing. It might involve choosing to stop working in a particular area.

Phil's Story

Phil has severe Parkinson's Syndrome. He works as a psychiatrist in private practice. He's worried about his medical deterioration and wonders how much longer he'll be able to treat patients in his practice. Fortunately, as a psychiatrist, he needs to be able to think and speak clearly and isn't called upon to do subtle motor activity that could pose a significant problem if his disease worsens. He consults with a colleague on a regular basis to assess his functioning and his ability to maintain competence as a practicing psychiatrist.

Conclusion

This chapter focused on the need to be competent in your professional and personal life in order to be ethical. It's challenging to achieve competence in many areas and even harder to maintain it. Research clearly indicates that most people who are incompetent are not aware that they are incompetent, and it's difficult for us to judge our level of skill in most areas. Therefore, we need to have objective criteria for competence as well as a way to obtain regular corrective feedback. In order to cope with inevitable lapses in our competencies, we need to maintain integrity by being honest and fair with both ourselves and others in order to work hard to achieve and maintain competence and let go of the competencies that we cannot maintain.

Achieving and maintaining competence in both small and big areas of your life will require some ethical muscle. It can cost you a great deal if you are truly honest with yourself about your competencies. You can potentially lose a job, be embarrassed, and lose respect from others by being honest with your self and others about your competencies.

Test Yourself

Use what you have learned to make tough ethical decisions.

1. Your boss thinks you are more competent than you are and has given you a promotion over others in your company who you know are better qualified for the position. Do you take the promotion? Do you say anything about the qualifications of others? Why or why not?

2. You are nominated and elected to be the president of a social, civic, or church organization. You think that this is an honor and you are pleased and honored by the election results. However, you know that the person who lost the election would be much more competent to do the job and would be better for the organization. What do you do?

3. Your spouse exaggerates your competence and accomplishments at social gatherings with family and friends. Do you correct the exaggerations? Why or why not?

CHAPTER 5

Responsibility

"The devil made me do it." You've likely heard this excuse before. It was popularized by comedian Flip Wilson in the 1960s. It reflects what seems to be a pervasive and growing behavioral pattern among people that might be characterized by the cry, "It's not my fault!"

Refusing to take responsibility for your own actions seems to be the norm in recent years. The headlines are full of politicians, corporate executives, professional sports figures, celebrities, and members of the general public who do bad things, make poor judgments, and engage in unethical or illegal behavior, yet blame others or special circumstances for their actions.

Criminal Behavior and Guilty Pleas

Each day there are articles in the newspaper that report that someone was accused of a serious crime. The entered plea is almost always "not guilty." How often does a defendant plead guilty? How often does someone who committed a crime say, "Yes, I did it"? They may argue that there were circumstances that contributed to a crime, such as a misunderstanding, passion, jealousy, a compelling need for food, drugs, shelter, or revenge. But, how often does a defendant take responsibility for what he or she did? Of course, innocent people do in fact get accused of crimes. Innocent people do in fact go to jail for crimes that they haven't committed. However, it is rare that someone actually takes responsibility for the criminal actions that they engaged in. When a defendant does take responsibility there is usually a compelling excuse to justify the behavior (poverty, prejudice, substance abuse, divorced parents). By offering an excuse, they're actually saying that they really aren't truly responsible for their behavior, even if they admit that they committed the crime.

One of the most amazing examples of this is what has been referred to as the "Twinkie defense." In this famous 1978 case, Dan White, a former San Francisco county supervisor, shot and killed George Moscone, then mayor of San Francisco, and Harvey Milk, a San Francisco supervisor and gay activist. One of the explanations that was provided for the double murder was that Dan White ate too much junk food, which altered his judgment. So, while he admitted to the killings, he (or his defense attorney) claimed that he wasn't responsible since he was under the influence of junk food.

In the news, we see many examples of blaming poor behavior on everyone and everything other than the actual person who committed the problematic behavior. While there may be many legitimate factors that contribute to unethical, illegal, immoral, and criminal behavior, ultimately someone decides to act in a certain way. Rarely (if at all) does the devil make you do it.

This chapter will focus on responsibility. Taking responsibility is perhaps a declining and lost virtue for most people. We tend to want to take responsibility for good things ("I passed the exam because I studied hard and am smart") but not for failure ("I failed the exam because the instructor is a jerk and the test was unfair"). To be ethical we need to strive towards taking responsibility for our decisions and behavior (both good and bad). This chapter will discuss responsibility in some detail and try to create a plan to be more attentive and proactive in being ethically responsible.

What Does Being Responsible Mean?

Being responsible means being accountable and following through on your promises and obligations. Being responsible involves maintaining a social contract with others. It means fulfilling your duties. It generally means that you control your behavior and decisions and are thus responsible for what you do and say. While a variety of external factors might contribute to your thoughts and behaviors, being responsible means that you don't attribute your actions to the devil or to anything or anyone else. In practical terms, what do we mean by being responsible in everyday life? This depends on the various roles you play in life and in society.

Being a Responsible Worker

As an employee, you're expected to be responsible by showing up to work each day on time and by being ready to do your job. You're expected to be competent in your job and to be responsible for your work tasks and assignments. Companies are expected to be responsible to their customers, employees, and the community at large. However, a recent poll reported in the newspapers stated that half of all American workers claim that they have behaved in an unethical manner at work and generally cited job pressures for the reason (Ethics Officer Association. American Society of Chartered Life Underwriters and Chartered Financial Consultants. 1997). The collapse of giant companies such as Enron, Tyco, WorldCom, and Arthur Anderson underscore the irresponsible and unethical behavior that's sometimes the norm in corporate America. It's been cynically stated that "business ethics" is an oxymoron. What's our responsibility as workers?

What about whistle-blowers at work? What's our responsibility to report problem behaviors among our coworkers or superiors? For example, suppose you work in the airline industry. You notice that a coworker who deals with matters of safety is drunk or incompetent in some way. What do you do? Do you have some responsibility to inform authorities about what you've witnessed? Do you inform the coworker that he or she should get help or let someone else take over? Suppose you do inform authorities and your concerns are ignored or even ridiculed? Do you have a responsibility to do more? Do you go to the press with your concerns? Do you quit your job? How far does your responsibility go?

The dilemma described above is an extreme case. Irresponsibility in this example could result in people dying. Many similar examples of irresponsibility among coworkers or employers may not have such tragic outcomes. No one is likely to die if an employee at a clothing store is chronically late for work or isn't adequately familiar with the merchandise in the store. How might you deal with your responsibility as a coworker if fellow workers are acting irresponsibly but no one is likely to get hurt or killed?

Being a Responsible Steward of the Earth

What about our responsibility to the earth? As you know, Americans use more than their fair share of natural resources and contribute more than their share of pollution given the number of Americans (about 281 million) compared to the 6 billion people who live on the earth. Most of us likely drive cars that pollute the air, use household products (lawn fertilizer, pesticides) that pollute the water, use Styrofoam cups and many other disposable products (diapers, eating utensils, cameras) that add to the waste fills across the country. Much recent attention has been given to the popular proliferation of gas guzzling Sport Utility Vehicles (SUVs) and their impact on the environment. While no one individual's decision to use a car (rather than a bike, for example) for a given errand, buy a SUV (rather than a more energy efficient smaller car), or use a particular disposable household product (such as plastic razors) will significantly impact the environmental problems of the earth, such decisions made by many individuals add up to great impact. How responsible should we be for our choices and lifestyle in terms of their impact on the planet? How hard should we work to tread more lightly? Again, there are no simple answers.

Being a Responsible Human Being

What is our responsibility to other human beings in times of need? For example, suppose you witness an accident on the freeway. It looks like injuries may have occurred. The accident appears more serious than a minor fender bender. What do you do? Do you stop and see if you can help? Do you use a cell phone (if you have one) to call 911? Would you behave differently if you were driving on a very busy freeway with numerous other motorists than if you were driving on a freeway in a very rural area where there appear to be no other drivers? Social psychology research has been conducted on these and similar situations. You're more likely to stop and try and to help if you're driving on a rural freeway than if you are driving on a busy freeway because you feel more responsible to help if others are not around.

A few weeks ago while out of town on a business trip, I found myself waiting with my six-year-old son in our car in the parking lot of a supermarket. My wife was inside picking up a few items. A woman parked next to my car and went into the market. She left an approximately three-year-old girl alone in the car. The girl began to cry. She got out of the locked car and began to walk across the busy parking lot towards the market. What was my responsibility to the little girl as I witnessed these events unfold? What was my responsibility to my six-year-old boy who is in my car? I needed to make a quick decision. Should I leave my car (and my son unattended) to help this little girl? Should I attend to my child and ignore the distressed little girl? Should I bring my son with me while I attend to the little girl? In a split second, I decided that I had a responsibility to the little girl and left my car to attend to her. I told my son to wait for me while I tried to quickly make sure that a car in the busy parking lot didn't hit the girl. I felt that I couldn't bring my son because it would only take a moment for the little girl to get hit by a car. With an eye on my son in my car, I took the little girl to the door of the market where she saw her mother and ran towards her. I then quickly ran back to my car to attend to my child.

There are many issues of responsibility posed in this example. I have a responsibility to care for my child and not leave him unattended in the car. I felt that I had some responsibility to ensure that a car in the parking lot didn't hit the young girl as she tried to find her mother. You might ask what kind of mother would leave her three-year-old unattended in a car while she went shopping. The mother behaved in what appeared to be an irresponsible manner. What should I do about that? Should I speak with her about it? Should I call the police? I did none of that. I returned to my son as soon as the girl was safely with her mother.

What is our responsibility to others who have less than we do? One Princeton University professor wrote an op-ed piece in the *New York Times* (Singer 1999) suggesting that we have a moral responsibility to give all of our extra resources to organizations such as Oxfam to help feed the hungry across the world. He suggested that all money that might be used for nonessential things (vacations, movies, fancy coffee drinks, dinners out) should be directed to helping those with the most need. While few, if any, people would take their responsibility to help others to this extreme, it does bring up an important question about how far we should go to be responsible for the welfare of others. On the one hand, it may be irresponsible to do nothing to help when someone is in terrible need. However, few of us are willing to sell all we have and give it to the poor. This brings up the issue of what is good enough responsibility?

What Is Good Enough Responsibility?

How much responsibility should we take on to make the world a better place? We obviously cannot work to correct every wrong that we encounter in life. Realistically, we likely remain silent when we witness a coworker or boss do something wrong or act in an irresponsible manner. Sometimes we drive our cars when we could walk or bike instead. Sometimes we use Styrofoam cups. Sometimes we don't investigate all of the issues before voting. Sometimes we go on vacation rather than giving the money to Oxfam. The point here in listing these examples isn't to make you feel guilty or to make you feel that you have the weight of the world's problems on your shoulders. The purpose is for you to consider your minimum level of responsibility in the various areas in your life. The purpose is to encourage you to be attentive and mindful of efforts to be responsible for your actions. How do you know what good enough responsibility might be? Again, there are no easy answers to this question. You have to discover for yourself how responsible you should be, not only for your own actions but also for helping others.

In the many roles in your life you might be expected, at the minimum, to keep your promises and to acknowledge and correct your errors and wrongdoings. You might be expected to be responsible for yourself and not make excuses for irresponsible behavior. What you do beyond that must be your choice in trying to live an ethical life. The tough ethical decisions emerge when you're taking responsibility for yourself and your actions cost you a great deal. For example, taking responsibility for a crime you committed might result in your going to jail. Taking responsibility for reporting unethical or illegal actions at work might result in your losing your job and becoming a scapegoat. You can use the various approaches to ethics (utilitarian, common good, justice, values, and so on) that were discussed earlier to help guide your criteria of what is good enough responsibility for you.

How Do You Know If You Are Responsible?

As mentioned in the last chapter, it's not so easy to judge ourselves. Most people would, when asked, state that they're ethical and responsible people. Very few would admit to being irresponsible. Yet, many of these "responsible" people would use all sorts of reasons and excuses to account for their irresponsible behavior. So, accurate self-knowledge isn't always so easy to assess. If we're such poor judges of our own behavior, how can we tell if we're being responsible or irresponsible?

While there are no simple answers, some useful principles and exercises can serve as a guide.

EXERCISE 5.1

Here's an exercise to make this discussion more concrete and relevant to your life. Write down five things that you have done that you're not proud of. What have you done that you feel might have been unethical, immoral, illegal, cruel, and so forth? What have you done that you now regret? Perhaps you lied to someone or stole something. Perhaps you had an angry outburst and said some very mean things to someone close to you. Perhaps you got angry on the freeway and really expressed your anger towards another driver in hurtful ways. Maybe you deceived someone for your own personal gain. Think about the five things that you've said or done that you now believe, in hindsight, were irresponsible.

Now, next to each item on your list, write down exactly why you behaved as you did. What is your reasoning to explain your behavior? How do you understand behaving in this way? Write these reasons down. Be honest with yourself.

Next, review the reasons that you noted. What themes emerge? Did you behave as you did because of an abusive childhood experience? Did you behave as you did due to a misunderstanding? Did you behave as you did because you watch too much television or drink too much alcohol? Did you behave as you did because the devil made you do it?

You might also ask someone you know and trust to offer an explanation for your behavior. You might get a second opinion about why you did what you did.

What have you learned about yourself in this exercise? Do you tend to take responsibility for your actions or do you blame others? Do you tend to think that your behavior is due to a traumatic past, a challenging present circumstance, the influence of society, of your parents, or of your peers?

Double Standards

As discussed in the previous chapter, we often use a double standard when evaluating how responsible we should be. We tend to take responsibility for our own good behavior and good outcomes and avoid responsibility for bad behavior or bad outcomes. We're more likely to judge others more harshly when it comes to responsibility than we judge ourselves or those we're close to and love.

Perhaps you have personally engaged in a serious and problematic behavior such as alcoholism, drunk driving, shoplifting, beating a child or spouse, or some other problem behavior. How do you explain yourself? Do you take full responsibility, or do you blame your behavior on others or on special circumstances?

The point here is that we might have a set of standards regarding responsibility that we apply to others (especially people we don't know or don't like) and another set of standards that we apply to ourselves or to those we love. The exact same behavior committed by a stranger might get a very different reaction from you than it would if committed by a loved one.

How Can You Become More Responsible For Yourself?

How can we appropriately and accurately maintain the ethical goal of being responsible? How do we make tough ethical decisions by maintaining appropriate responsibility for our actions when taking responsibility will cost us a great deal? Of course, we can't be responsible for everything. There are many things and events that we aren't responsible for and we shouldn't take any responsibility for. For example, a woman named Betty reported a funny story about her son that happened following a large 7.1 earthquake in the San Francisco Bay area during October 1989. As Betty's home was shaking violently she ran to the outside door and called for her son Jimmy. "Jimmy!" she yelled. Her then five-year-old son cried out, "Mom, I didn't do it!" Clearly, Jimmy wasn't responsible for the 7.1 earthquake.

Sadly, some people do in fact take on more responsibility than they should. For example, some people blame themselves for getting sick with diseases that may have nothing to do with their behavior. Of course, some cancers have been linked to lifestyle (some forms of skin and lung cancer), but many cancers appear to be related to genetic predisposition, genetic mutations due to unknown causes, unknown exposure to toxins, and factors unrelated to personal behavior.

Most people are more likely to avoid feeling responsible for things. Many shirk their responsibilities or provide excuses for irresponsible behavior. So how can we be appropriately responsible? Like most ethical questions raised in this book, there are no easy answers. However, there are some guiding principles that can be of help.

Own It

You might ask, "Why do I want to take responsibility?" It's much easier to shirk responsibility for our actions when it's convenient or in our interest to do so. Admitting our errors, faults, and poor judgments and decisions isn't very appealing. Why do it? To live an ethical life and make good tough ethical decisions we need to take responsibility for our thoughts and behavior.

Now, as the saying goes, "Rome was not built in a day." You may not be able to be more responsible about your thoughts and behavior overnight. You may even choose to make excuses and blame others for your behavior during certain moments. However, you likely will make little if any progress on living more ethically if you don't work on being more responsible for your behavior. It might be useful trying to keep the big picture in mind (the value of living an ethical life) when confronted with situations that tempt you to shirk responsibility.

No self-help book can give you motivation to change. You've got to want it. This book can assist you, but ultimately you need to want to make the effort. Perhaps an exercise can help you better see the advantages (and disadvantages) of being responsible for your actions.

EXERCISE 5.2

Make a list of five behaviors that you engage in or have engaged in when you avoided responsibility. Perhaps these might include drinking, not adequately supervising your children, driving recklessly, hurting a friend or family member, or avoiding visiting a sick colleague. Now, write the advantages to avoiding responsibility on each of these occasions. For example, you might say that if you don't admit that you were hurtful to a friend then you don't have to feel guilty. You might say that if you don't take responsibility for drunk driving you don't have to admit that you have a drinking problem. Once you complete the list of advantages, then write down a list of disadvantages of avoiding responsibility. These might include not being honest with yourself or with others. It might include living a lie.

What have you learned about yourself in this exercise? Do the advantages of avoiding responsibility outweigh the disadvantages?

EXERCISE 5.3

List at least five reasons why you should take responsibility for your behavior. Perhaps you want to be a good role model for your children or be able to live with yourself better. Can you come up with five reasons? Do they seem compelling to you? Rate how compelling each of your reasons is, using a scale of 1 to 10, in which 1 is not compelling at all and 10 is highly compelling. How compelling are your reasons to take responsibility?

Get Feedback

People who know you best such as family, friends, or coworkers can help you get a better sense of how responsible or irresponsible you are about things in your life. For example, I'm sure that you know people in your life who are irresponsible but may not even know it.

John is a psychologist working in a large practice. He is often late for his appointments with his patients. Furthermore, he has occasionally fallen asleep during treatment sessions. He also does some supervision with graduate students in psychology. He frequently upsets them with his rigid views about how to best evaluate and treat clinical patients. When confronted about his behavior by his boss, John seemed clueless that he'd done anything wrong. He sincerely seemed surprised that anyone would think that he was behaving inappropriately. Luckily, John was open about the feedback and worked hard to change his irresponsible behavior.

John's boss took some risk in confronting John. Providing people with negative corrective feedback can be unpleasant and upsetting. Suppose John got angry with his boss and lashed out at him? John's boss did the right thing, but it could have cost him a great deal if John had reacted poorly.

We all know people like John. They may mean well, but they don't always act in a responsible manner. John didn't even think that his behavior was problematic or irresponsible. Nonetheless, he must be made aware of the problem in order to fix it. Even if no really bad outcomes occur, the behavior still needs attention.

So, how can you be sure that you're behaving in a responsible manner? One way is for you to try and get objective feedback from others who know you well.

EXERCISE 5.4

Think about the people in your life who know you best. Write their names down. Try to think of at least five people. Ask them to tell you what ways they think you are responsible and what ways they think you are irresponsible. Ask them to be honest with you and not to worry about hurting your feelings (assuming this is true and you believe that you can receive the feedback without being angry or defensive once you get it). Listen to their feedback without any commentary or excuses.

What have you learned from this exercise? Do the people who know you best think you are irresponsible in some ways? Perhaps they feel that you don't answer phone calls or e-mail messages promptly. Perhaps they feel that you don't keep the house clean enough. Perhaps they feel that you drive irresponsibly. Perhaps they believe you blame your problems and shortcomings on others? Are there themes that have emerged from their feedback? What are they?

In order to understand our strengths and weaknesses in terms of responsibility, we must have accurate and objective feedback. Can you get it? If you can get it, can you listen to it without being defensive?

Can You Hear Feedback?

Once you get feedback, you need to be able to hear it without getting overly defensive. This is no easy task. As mentioned earlier, our initial reaction to criticism or corrective feedback is generally to defend ourselves. We have all sorts of reasons to reject the feedback we hear. To be fair, not all feedback is objective and accurate. People may be entitled to their opinions, but there's certainly no guarantee that there opinions are correct. So you must take all of the feedback that you receive and somehow determine if it's accurate or not. How can you do this?

First, you might want to pay close attention to feedback that comes from several different people all basically saying the same thing. For example, if a number of people independently tell you that you're an irresponsible driver or parent or coworker, you can be more assured that this feedback, although perhaps hard to hear and accept, is likely to be accurate. This is why you should ask five people who know you well for feedback and not just one person.

Second, you might pay close attention to objective data that helps you to determine if you're responsible. For example, if you have a lot of speeding tickets or have been involved in numerous traffic accidents, or perhaps have had a DUI violation, the odds are high that you may not be a responsible driver. If you've forgotten to pick up your friend at the airport after promising that you would do so on several occasions, you might be an irresponsible (or certainly unreliable) friend. The more objective the data, the better. Relying on the opinions of others without objective data is subject to too much potential bias. It's harder to be defensive when you have objective data to work with.

How do you generally react when someone provides you with corrective feedback? Are you defensive? If you become aware of your tendency towards defensiveness, you may be better able to avoid behaving this way in the future. Asking others if they find you to be defensive might help you as well.

Watch Others Who Do It Well

It's easier to be responsible if you have a model to emulate. Think of people who you know or have heard about who have taken responsibility for their behavior. Have you known people who have been confronted by others about a serious error in judgment or a bad decision? Perhaps right when you expected them to provide a ratio-nale or excuse, they surprised you with their honesty and their efforts to take responsibility for their behavior. If you've ever wit-nessed such an interaction, it's often refreshing to see someone who chooses not to make excuses or blame others but actually takes responsibility for what they did.

EXERCISE 5.5

Think of someone you know (or have heard of) who is a good model of responsibility. What did they do or say that made you feel that they were responsible? Do they serve as a good model for you?

Think of the different roles that you have in your life (parent, employee, driver, and citizen). Write down a model of a highly responsible person in each of the roles that you have in life. For example, who is an excellent example or model of a responsible parent? Who do you consider an excellent example of a responsi-ble worker in your line of work? What makes you think that each of these models or examples are such good examples of being responsible? What do they do or say that make you believe that they're good models for you?

What have you learned from these exercises? Can these examples be models for you?

Get Support

Many people who benefit from self-help groups such as Alcoholics Anonymous, Sexaholic Anonymous, and similar groups report that they appreciate the way fellow members can help them avoid making excuses and shirking responsibility for their actions. Surrounding yourself with people who can help you be responsible and model responsible behavior is very helpful. Can you surround yourself with such people?

You may not want to join a support group, but you may be able to surround yourself with people who are responsible. There may also be church or civic groups you can join whose members share your values. You can nurture friendships with like-minded responsible people. Perhaps some people in your life are poor influences on you in terms of responsibility. Research tells us that people usually compare their behavior with those around them. So, if you surround yourself with poor models who behave in an irresponsible manner, you're more likely to behave as they do. An exercise might help you evaluate those who can help and support you and your efforts to be more responsible.

EXERCISE 5.6

Think of the people in your life. Are they generally responsible or irresponsible? List five ways that you can increase your circle of responsible friends and coworkers. Is this something you can do?

Have a Plan

In order to be more responsible, you need a game plan. How will you accomplish your goal of being more responsible? What specific things must you do? What areas of your life do you need to take more responsibility for? Perhaps an exercise can help you outline a plan to become more responsible for your actions.

EXERCISE 5.7

List five areas in your life where you could improve your responsibility. Write them down. Perhaps you might include your role at work or at home. You might include your role as a citizen, community member, or caretaker of the earth's resources. For each area, what specific things can you do to make progress? List them. How will you know if you have made progress? What criteria can you use to assess yourself? What kind of feedback do you need to ensure that you are on the right track?

What has this exercise taught you? Do you feel that you have identified areas of your life where you could be more responsible? Do you have a workable game plan?

Conclusion

This chapter focused on responsibility. In order for you to do the right thing and live a more ethical life you must be responsible for your thoughts, feelings, and behaviors. How we deal with errors also matters. Working on being more responsible for both the good and the bad behaviors that we engage in is a big step. In order to make tough ethical decisions, we need to take responsibility for ourselves and strive to minimize defensive behavior. This provides a foundation to help you with the next few steps of living an ethical life. Thus far, this book has focused on the ethical principles of integrity, competence, and responsibility. These are characteristics that we, for the most part, work on in ourselves. The next two chapters will focus on ethical issues that relate to our treatment of others. Chapter 6 will focus on respect for others' rights and dignity, and chapter 7 will focus on concern for the welfare of others.

Test Yourself

Use what you have learned to make tough ethical decisions.

1. You run over and accidentally kill a dog with your car on your way to an important meeting at work. You are running late. The dog has an identification tag. Do you contact the owners? If so, when? Why or why not?

2. You made a big error at work that cost the company a big sale. You know that you are responsible for the problem, but no one else does. Do you admit your error? Why or why not?

3. You cut someone off on the freeway, which results in a traffic accident between several cars but not yours. Do you stop and accept responsibility, or do you drive off? Why or why not?

CHAPTER 6

Respect

Perhaps you've been told to "pay some respect" at some point in your life. You're more likely to have heard someone say that to you when you were perceived as not being appropriately or adequately polite or deferential. Perhaps you've told someone else to "pay some respect." But what does respect really mean?

Respect means treating others with esteem, consideration, and honor. Respect involves treating others with attention and acknowledging that they have rights and needs as well. Respect means being considerate and appreciative of others. Respect means treating others as you'd want to be treated.

Although respect involves how we treat other people, it also involves how we treat animals, plants, buildings, and property in general, and our environment. Respect involves how we interact with both living and nonliving things.

Respect for Life

Many people strive to respect and value all life. Our hearts sink when we hear news about people getting killed in accidents, by criminals, or by distraught loved ones. We tend to be especially upset when children die. Tragically, a murder-suicide report where a distraught man kills his wife (or former wife or perhaps girlfriend) and their children and then kills himself is all too commonly reported in the news. Senseless deaths and accidents seem particularly upsetting. Our interest and sadness about these events are at least partially related to our belief that life is sacred, valuable, and should be respected.

Maintaining a strong respect for life often leads to vigorous political debates. For example, many people in the United States and abroad are morally or religiously opposed to abortion. The phrases "respect life" and "right to life" are often used among people who try to eliminate or at least minimize abortions. They often feel that we should respect human life and not terminate a pregnancy for any reason. Some people are opposed to eating meat because they feel that the lives of animals aren't being adequately respected. Many argue that eating meat isn't necessary to maintain life and health and so people shouldn't kill animals when they can live comfortably as a vegetarian.

This chapter will focus on respect as one of the five ethical principles to live by. Specifically, it will focus on respect for other people's rights and dignity. To live an ethical life we must be respectful of others. How can we live ethically if we don't respect others? How do we respect people's rights and their dignity when we don't like them or we disagree with what they do or say? Should we be respectful of murderers, terrorists, and child molesters? If so, how? These are some of the challenging questions that will be discussed in this chapter.

Contemporary Problems with Lack of Respect

One way to develop a better understanding of what respect means is to examine some contemporary problems with lack of respect. There are numerous examples of people failing to show respect for people and property. Are people less respectful today than in the past? It's difficult to answer this question. However, many people have noted that lack of respect is a common problem in contemporary life.

Lack of Civility in Public

Much attention has been paid to the lack of civil behavior in public. One example is road rage, these are cases of people expressing frustration by behaving in an angry manner towards fellow drivers. Stories of people shouting obscenities or threatening others are common. There have been stories in the news of people using guns and other deadly weapons after minor fender benders.

Another example is when parents behave rudely towards other parents during sports events where their children are competing. There have been some notable cases of rage where people have even been killed. A recent example includes a forty-year-old man in the Boston area who got into a fight with a fellow parent at a hockey game. The fight ended with one of the dads being beaten to death. While this is a dramatic and tragic example, a lot of attention has been focused on sports rage, road rage, office rage, and so forth. In all of these examples, a lack of civility and respectful behavior was displayed towards others.

Lack of Respect in the Service Industries

Most people in service-related businesses often tell stories of being treated in a highly disrespectful and rude manner by customers. Cashiers, waiters, and clerks at retail stores usually have many stories about people behaving in rude, insulting, demanding, and, ultimately, disrespectful and unethical ways.

These few examples highlight how commonly a lack of respect can occur in contemporary society. From children calling adults by their first names to people getting killed in road rage incidents, lack of respect is a common problem in both small and big ways. You can probably think of many other examples as well. How can we work to behave towards others in a more respectful manner? There are no easy answers to this question, but behaving towards others with respect can help us live a more ethical life.

Five Principles to Live More Respectfully

As we strive toward living life in a more respectful manner, five principles emerge that can help guide us. Think of these ideals as guidelines for living more respectfully.

1. All people are worthy of respect.

2. Treat others as you wish to be treated.

3. People are entitled to their opinions and decisions even if they are wrong.

4. Even if you feel rage, anger, or hate, you don't need to express it.

5. It's easier to be respectful when you can forgive.

Principle 1: All People Are Worthy of Respect

In order to embrace respect as one of our five ethical principles for living, we need to accept several important assumptions. First, we need to embrace the notion that all people (and perhaps all living things) are worthy of respect. The major religious traditions teach that since God created all things and can be found in all things, then we should treat all things with respect. In this way of thinking, respect for people and other living things is actually demonstrating respect for God. This belief tends to view life as sacred due to God's influence in creating and sustaining life. People who aren't affiliated with a religious tradition or don't believe in any particular deity may also feel that all life is sacred for different reasons and therefore believe that all life and all people should be treated with respect (with or without God).

While it may be fairly easy to agree that all life should be treated with respect, several problems with this assumption emerge immediately. First, we need to be clearer about what we mean by treating life and others with respect. Exactly how do we treat others with respect? What's respectful behavior and what's disrespectful behavior? What's good enough respect? In other words, what's the minimal level of respect I should show towards others? Second, should all living things be treated with respect equally? For example, should people who have committed horrific crimes be treated with the same amount of respect as the pillars of our society? Is there a minimum level of respect we should show towards all living creatures but a higher level or amount of respect provided to others who we admire for who they are and what they do? Some cultures do this naturally. For example, the Japanese culture includes demonstrating respect for others by the frequency and intensity of bowing when you interact with others (especially when saying hello and goodbye).

What Do We Mean by Treating Others with Respect?

This is certainly not an easy question to answer. Reasonable and ethical people may sincerely have very different views about what is and what is not respectful behavior. Here's an exercise to help you apply the principle of respect to your daily interactions with others.

What has this exercise taught you? Do you have a better sense of specific behaviors that are both respectful and disrespectful? You might also ask someone you know well and trust to list disrespectful behaviors that they witness from you. Perhaps your friend, coworker, spouse, sister, or partner might view you as behaving in a disrespectful manner when you believe that you are acting perfectly fine.

You may wonder how saying "hello" and "please" is related to making tough ethical decisions. Again, if we're comfortable and used to treating all people with respect in our daily lives, we're more likely to treat others with respect when it really counts. It might be very difficult to treat someone you don't like with respect. It might be very challenging to treat property or all living things with respect when it will cost you to do so. It might be really tough to act respectfully toward someone you don't like or who has hurt you in some significant way. If you can manage this in small ways, you have a better chance of managing respect in large ways.

Good Enough or Minimum Respect

It's often difficult to treat people we don't know or like with respect. This is where tough ethical decision making comes into play. For example, what amount of respect would you demonstrate towards a terrorist, a murderer, or a rapist? What kind of respect would you have towards a criminal who has hurt you or someone you love? What kind of respect would you show towards someone who has cheated you or has lied to you about something really important?

A remarkable story of respect and forgiveness emerged from the horrible Rodney King verdict riots in Los Angeles in 1992. You may remember the beating that Reginald Denny, an innocent truck driver, received after being pulled out of his cab. This terrible beating was recorded by the media and repeatedly played across the world. After he healed from his serious head injury, he testified at the trial of those accused of beating him. He showed an amazing level of respect and forgiveness toward those who savagely beat him. He embraced the parents of the accused as well. This is an excellent example of making a tough ethical decision that involves respect for others. Few of us would have been as forgiving and caring as Reginald Denny. Maybe very few of us would have made the tough decision to be so respectful to someone who had hurt us.

What is the minimum level of respect we should give to strangers on the street or to people we know well but don't like? The ideals of the American justice system suggest that everyone (no matter how heinous they are) is worthy of being considered innocent until proven guilty and are worthy of a fair trial. While it's debatable if these ideals are followed in reality in all cases, they suggest that everyone deserves at least a minimum level of respect. In our society, the most despicable criminals are (theoretically at least) given regular meals, allowed to use the restroom as needed, aren't tortured, abused or harassed, and are provided with free legal counsel if needed. So, living ethically suggests that everyone should be treated with at least a minimum degree of respect.

Although defining actual respectful and disrespectful behaviors isn't easy and will involve many individual differences of opinions, most people would likely agree that certain minimal respectful behaviors should be provided for all. In general, treating others with minimal respect means being polite, avoiding angry name calling and insults, being sensitive to the needs, feelings, and interests of others, not hitting others, taking the opinions of others (even if you disagree with these opinions) into consideration. Respect means saying "please" and "thank you" when appropriate. Of course, exactly how you treat others with respect depends on whom you're interacting with. How you behave in a respectful manner with a child might differ from how you're respectful towards a coworker or a sales clerk. How you behave in a respectful manner with a child molester might be very different from how you behave toward your best friend or your mother. Different people might require or demand different levels of respect. However, as illustrated in the case of Reginald Denny, all people, regardless of who they are or what they have done, might be treated with a great deal of respect. Here's an exercise to help you get a better feel for the minimal level of respect you should provide to others in your life.

EXERCISE 6.1

Think of the people that you regularly interact with who usually get very little respect. Perhaps these people might include a telephone solicitor, a homeless person on the street who asks for spare change as you pass by, a janitor or gas station attendant, or a stranger. Who in your life tends to get little respect? List at least five people who get little respect in your life. Now, write down the exact behaviors that you should engage in to provide these people with a minimal level of respect. What behaviors do you think demonstrate a minimal level of respect? Might these include greeting someone with a "hello" and "goodbye?" Might it include answering their questions or saying "no thank you" when they want something from you that you don't want to give? Be specific. Are you rude or abrupt with these people? Do you ignore them as if they don't exist?

What have you learned from this exercise? Do you have a sense of your minimal obligation to provide people with respect?

Too often people don't show respect to many people whom they come into contact with on a daily basis. This might include strangers, fellow drivers, sale clerks, homeless people begging on the street, and people they view as less important. A woman was trying to get service at an upscale supermarket deli the other day. She appeared frustrated because no one working at the deli seemed to notice that she was in need of attention. After waiting a few moments, she asked in a rude tone, "Is anyone actually working here?" She treated the workers at the deli without respect. She could've gotten someone's attention in a more respectful manner by asking, for example, "Can someone please help me?" Rather, she was demeaning and rude, due to her frustration at not being served promptly.

When you are frustrated or angry, it's very difficult to take the extra moment to select your words and tone carefully in order to speak respectfully. In fact, when you are angry, you are probably at your most vulnerable for treating others disrespectfully. Your impulse might be to express your anger and frustration directly, with little if any appropriate filtering. Perhaps some events justify this type of response. For example, if you catch someone stealing your car, you might yell at the thief in angry tones without worrying too much about being disrespectful to him or her. However, in general, the anger and frustration that we experience and fail to filter occurs with fellow drivers, our children, spouse, partner, sales clerks, and so forth. We must remember to show at least a minimum level of respect to all humans if we're trying to live more ethically.

Principle 2: Treat Others As You Would Wish to Be Treated

A second important assumption that we need to accept to live more respectfully is the notion that treating others as we wish to be treated is a worthy and noble goal. In order to treat others as we wish to be treated, we need to have some empathy for others. We need to have some sense of what it might feel like being in someone else's shoes. Unfortunately, for may people, it's not always easy to experience empathy for others. There are many people who have very little empathy for others. They truly don't really know what it might be like living in someone else's skin. Without empathy, it would be very difficult, if not impossible, to be able to treat everyone with respect.

Some might argue that this principle sets too high a standard, but one of the most important ways that we can ensure that everyone we interact with is treated with respect is to act on this principle. Having some empathy for others can help us accomplish this goal. How can we develop empathy for others? What must we do to feel that we have some sense of what it might be like to be someone else?

EXERCISE 6.2

Look over the list you created in exercise 6.1. Review the list of people you interact with on a regular basis who generally do not get much respect. Again, this list might include a homeless person, a telemarketer, a sales clerk, a cleaning person, or others. Now, imagine yourself in each of these roles. Close your eyes and imagine yourself as a homeless person, for example. What would it be like? Imagine yourself in dirty clothes, hungry, tired, perhaps suffering from a psychiatric problem such as severe depression or substance abuse. Imagine that you have no place to sleep tonight and that it'll likely be very cold and uncomfortable sleeping in a doorway or on a sidewalk bench. Spend some time with this image.

Or if you wrote "cleaning person" on your list, imagine yourself working as a cleaning person in a hotel. Imagine spending your days cleaning the messes of others. Imagine having people ignore you or regularly treat you with little respect.

Do the same visualization activity for the other people you noted in exercise 6.1. While visualizing these images is a far cry from actually being these people, it at least gives you some sense of what it might be like to live in someone else's shoes. In doing so, some empathy should emerge.

It would be foolish to think that a brief exercise in this book would significantly change your sense of empathy for others. Hopefully, this exercise gives you a better sense of the challenging situation that others find themselves in. Ideally, spending some time with the people on your list would give you a better sense of their lives and thus more empathy.

If you conclude that you should treat others as you would wish to be treated, then you can develop strategies to ensure that you treat everyone with respect. For example, before you interact with someone (especially when you are angry or frustrated), you might want to put yourself in the other person's shoes and ask, "How would I want to be treated?" This question becomes the litmus test for social interactions. Alternatively, you might visualize or imagine that the person you're interacting with is actually someone you really respect and admire.

EXERCISE 6.3

For one day carefully observe all of your interactions with others. Try to imagine what it might be like being the person you are interacting with. With each interaction, ask yourself how you would want to be treated in this particular situation. Let the phrase "treat others as you would like to be treated" become your motto or mantra for the day. Consider writing down your impressions of your interactions during the course of the day.

Once you have completed this exercise consider the following questions. Did you treat people differently than you would normally treat them? Were you more respectful? Were you kinder to others? How did people respond to you? Did they respond differently than they usually do?

Principle 3: People Are Entitled to Their Opinions

We often treat people in a disrespectful manner when we feel that they're wrong about something. We all have opinions about all sorts of things. Some opinions can be clearly wrong. For example, someone might be of the opinion that the world is flat or that the Civil War never happened. Though these opinions are indeed wrong, some people might still hold onto them. How can we continue to respect people when we disagree with them?

While it might be easy to continue respecting someone when you disagree with them about something fairly minor (the best restaurant in town, the best movie or vacation spot) it may be harder to respect someone when you disagree with them about something that really matters to you. Sadly, too many people come to disrespect others who don't see things as they see them. Over the centuries, for example, many people have felt justified in killing others who don't share similar religious or political views.

Furthermore, a disagreement about some topic can quickly turn into disrespectful behavior. For example, a woman named Irene described a city council meeting where members of the community were discussing ways to slow traffic on a major road that went through town. Citizens expressed differing views about ways to slow traffic on the busy street. Some neighbors wanted to see traffic-slowing devices installed while others wanted more police presence on the street instead. As the debate grew and got more heated, tempers increased, and opinions got polarized. Irene was amazed that many people started to behave in a rude and disrespectful manner towards each other.

In order to live a more ethical life, we must continue to maintain at least a minimal level of respect for people, regardless of their opinions and decisions. Of course, we don't have to like others or agree with them about their views. However, treating others with respect, even when they're wrong, is needed to live ethically.

EXERCISE 6.4

Think of someone you know and respect but you generally disagree with on important matters. Perhaps there is someone you know who maintains very different political, religious, or other views that are difficult for you to agree with or accept. How do you maintain treating this person with respect? What behaviors do you engage in that are respectful? List them.

Now, think of someone you know who you find it very difficult to maintain respect for due to differences of opinion. Do you treat them with little or no respect? What behaviors do you engage in that are disrespectful? List them.

What have you learned from this exercise? Do you find it difficult to treat all people with respect even if they have thoughts or behaviors that you adamantly disagree with?

Principle 4: You Don't Have to Express Anger or Hate

Disagreeing with someone can certainly make you angry and even rageful if you disagree about something that's really important to you. It's fairly easy for many people to treat others in a disrespectful manner when they're very angry about something. Perhaps anger is one of the biggest risk factors for treating others without respect. Managing your anger will likely help you to live more ethically and help you treat others with respect.

For many years, mental health professionals and the general public believed that it was important to express your anger when the impulse struck you. The belief was that holding anger in was dangerous and unhealthy and thus you should let it out. Research in psychology has clearly demonstrated that these beliefs are unfounded (Bushman 2002). Research has shown that expressing anger in an unfiltered manner does not necessarily improve your psychological or physical well-being. In fact, it harms it. Therefore, when you feel anger you don't necessarily need to express it to maximize your physical and mental health (Bushman 2002).

There are many occasions when expressing anger might be appropriate and reasonable. The point isn't to stifle all expression of anger. The point is that anger can be expressed in a way that isn't productive for anyone and may easily lead to disrespectful and thus unethical behavior. When we get angry, we're less likely to think about maintaining respect for others or ethical behavior in general. Furthermore, if someone has trouble managing impulses in general or they have been drinking alcohol, adequately controlling anger may be especially challenging.

Although difficult for many to do, when we feel anger or frustration, we must deal with it in a way that maintains our respect for others. There are a variety of techniques that you can use to cope better with anger. In fact, there are a number of helpful self-help books available that specifically focus on anger management. The purpose here isn't to reiterate or summarize those books. Rather, you might work on managing anger in a way that highlights treating others with respect. Name-calling, hitting, screaming, saying cruel things, and so forth does not maintain respect for others. Taking a deep breath, focusing on the specific behaviors that you find troublesome, and offering corrective feedback in a way that maintains another's dignity is what you're encouraged to try to do. Tough ethical decisions emerge when hot issues stimulate you to angrily lash out at others.

What has this exercise taught you? Do you generally treat others with respect when you are angry? Do you say or do things when angry that are cruel, disrespectful, unproductive?

Principle 5: It's Easier to Be Respectful When You Can Forgive

It's easier to treat others with respect if we can work towards forgiving others. To forgive means to pardon, to excuse, and to renounce anger and bitterness.

Forgiving doesn't mean forgetting. You don't have to forget the awful things that someone else did. Forgiving doesn't mean that you either agree with the behavior of another person or that you can understand why they behaved as they did when they hurt you. Forgiveness doesn't mean that you have to like the person who hurt you. Forgiveness means letting go and moving on. Holding onto the anger and rage that comes with an inability to forgive ultimately hurts you and no one else. In fact, research has indicated that the ability to forgive is associated with a wide variety of positive mental and physical health outcomes (Luskin 2002).

If you have trouble forgiving others, then you must live with the daily frustration, anger, bitterness, and resentment that go along with the inability to forgive. Your blood pressure may rise, you may have trouble relaxing, and you might engage in health damaging behaviors such as drinking alcohol to excess or smoking cigarettes. Furthermore, you may find it more difficult to get and maintain social support because people generally don't want to be around someone who is angry and frustrated much of the time. Therefore, there are a variety of different behavioral and emotional pathways that might lead to mental and physical health troubles associated with being unable to forgive and let go.

Translating Ideals into Actual Behavior

Translating ideals into actual behavior isn't always easy. How can you turn the five principles about living in a more respectful manner into changed behavior on a day-to-day basis? You can use some of the same methods discussed in previous chapters.

Find Motivation

To treat others with respect, you've got to want to do it. This may be especially difficult if you have trouble being empathetic towards others or have trouble controlling your anger. If you've read this far in this book, you likely have a significant degree of motivation to live more ethically. In order to accomplish this goal, you need to want to treat all things with respect. While reading a self-help book might not give you the desire to do something, it hopefully gives you some tools to help you harness your motivation to accomplish your goal.

Observe Others

In order to treat others with respect, you need role models. You need to find others in your life that exemplify respectful behavior. In the Roman Catholic faith tradition, learning about the lives of the saints gives members of the faith some models for living a more faithful life. These models are extraordinary people who serve as best-case examples of faith-filled living. Who are some best-case examples for you to emulate? If you don't have any role models, can you find some?

Get Corrective Feedback

Sometimes we don't realize that we are behaving in a disrespectful or rude manner. Sometimes we need to obtain feedback from others to help get a better sense of our behavior. Again, getting objective and useful feedback from someone who is both knowledgeable and trustworthy is not always easy. Furthermore, sometimes it's hard to avoid being defensive. Who in your life can be relied on to provide useful feedback regarding respect? Can you avoid becoming defensive? How can you get feedback on a regular basis to keep your respectful behavior in check?

Surround Yourself with People of Like Mind

In order to live more respectfully towards others, you'll need support. Do you have friends, family, coworkers, and others in your life who also would like to live more ethically by being more respectful of others? If so, spend time with them so that you can reinforce and nurture each other in your efforts. Perhaps you can provide feedback to each other and come up with strategies to be more respectful. This is especially important when really tough ethical decisions come your way.

Conclusion

This chapter focused on treating all living things (especially people) with respect. In order for us to live more ethically, we need to maintain at least a minimal level of respect for all people and things. However, translating these ideals into actual behavior is challenging. Although it's hard, it's possible to do. You can learn to be more respectful towards others. If you're able to treat others as you would want to be treated, manage your anger, accept differences and find strategies to maximize a more respectful way of being with others, then you're ready for the last ethical principle discussed in the next chapter: concern for others.

Test Yourself

Use what you have learned to make tough ethical decisions.

1. You are in court for the trial of the person who is accused of raping your daughter. You accidentally bump into this person in the hallway during a recess. What do you do or say?

2. You are in the military and you are stationed in a country where women are not allowed to wear pants and expose their skin and hair. You are a female military person who is off duty for a day and you hoped to travel around town to see sites and so forth. How do you dress for the occasion?

3. You talk with a coworker over lunch about religious issues. You find that their religious beliefs seem bizarre, silly, and even offensive. Your coworker asks you what you think of his or her beliefs. What do you say?

CHAPTER 7

Concern

We live in narcissistic times. Many people seem to be concerned only about their own needs and interests and have little concern for others. Too many people can be demanding, entitled, self-centered, and self-absorbed. If the 1970s were the "me decade" then the 1980s and 1990s ended up being the "me decade" on steroids! We haven't come to a point where a "we" focus has emerged. How can we live an ethical life that involves concern for others when we're so focused on ourselves? This is the challenge that this chapter takes on.

Definitions

What does concern for others mean? Concern means care for, interest, and involvement in others. It suggests that others are important and worthy of attention. Concern suggests that in order to live an ethical life, you must be interested in the welfare of others. This makes good sense. How can you claim to be ethical if you're uninterested or oblivious to the needs and struggles of others? How can you be ethical if you're solely interested in yourself and your own self-interests?

How do we show concern for others? How does our concern for others translate into actual behavior? What is our ethical obligation to express concern for others who we don't know or like? How far should the ethical principle of concern for others go? Is there a minimal amount of concern that we should show to others? These are some of the many challenging questions that will be addressed in this chapter.

Concern for Others: A Matter of Degree

Most of us experience and express concern for the people we love. We're generally very interested in the welfare of our spouse, partner, children, parents, siblings, and friends. Obviously, we all likely experience and express more concern for some people in our lives than for others. For example, we might lose a good deal of sleep worrying about the welfare of our children but not for a distant cousin, a neighbor, or a stranger.

However, most of us likely experience and perhaps express concern for strangers as well. For example, we routinely hear stories in the media about terrible things that happen to people and animals. Often there is a public outpouring of concern expressed for strangers.

On the other hand, many people show very little concern to others in need. Too often we hear about starving children and families in various regions of the world. Too often we hear about people being abused, neglected, oppressed, and enslaved. Too often we hear about a homeless man or woman who dies on the street and is left there for hours before someone checks to see if he or she is all right. We can easily get desensitized to the various troubles people experience in the world after hearing daily stories of human suffering in the press. This is especially true when people who suffer don't seem to be like us in terms of culture, geographic location, age, gender, ethnicity, and other characteristics. If we seem to have little in common with those who suffer we may find it more challenging to feel or express concern for them.

It's certainly unreasonable to expect that we'd experience the same level of concern for all people and all living things. It's unlikely that our concern for strangers will approximate the concern we feel and express towards those we know and love. Thus, our level of concern for others is on a continuum from no concern to a great deal of concern depending upon the person and situation in question.

Yet, some people are able to muster up a tremendous amount of concern for everyone including strangers. Mother Teresa of Calcutta, India, was a good example of someone who showed a remarkable amount of concern for strangers in need. In addition to Mother Teresa, there are many much less famous people in the world who express concern for strangers on a daily basis and work to ease the suffering of all. People from all walks of life have made significant sacrifices in order to help others. Tragically, some have even died in their efforts to help strangers in need.

While it's certainly socially acceptable to express concern for others in need, you may not feel much concern for many of the people you know or feel much concern for strangers. A thirty-four-year old graduate student named Dick mentioned that he felt bad that he didn't feel more concern for people around him. He said he felt guilty that he felt so little when confronted with news that several people are struggling whom he knows. In fact, he admitted that he even enjoyed hearing about some of the misfortunes of others. He wondered if there might be something wrong with him since he didn't feel the level of concern for others that he believed that he should feel.

His feelings are likely to be fairly common. While most of us might not admit it to anyone, we may not feel concern towards many others and might even be pleased about some of the misfortunes of others. Terrible tragedies are reported each day in the daily news that involve murders, floods, earthquakes, traffic fatalities, child abductions, workplace and school shootings, and other horrific events. Many read these stories while relaxing with morning coffee. Even if concern is elicited by reading these horrific stories, it's usually momentary and fades away by the time the coffee cup is empty.

We naturally feel more concern for some people than for others. Before we discuss how we can enhance our concern for others, let's try an exercise to help you get a better sense of the concern you feel towards the people in your life.

EXERCISE 7.1

First, list the ten most important people in your life. These people might include your family members and closest friends. Then, using a scale of 1 to 10 where 1 equals no concern and 10 equals extreme concern, rate your level of concern for each of the ten people on your list. How much concern do you honestly feel about their welfare? Be honest with yourself.

Next, list ten people or groups of people that you regularly interact with but aren't on your list of the most important people in your life. This list could include co-workers, your boss, customers, neighbors, sale clerks you regularly interact with, and so forth. Now, use the same 1 to 10 scale to rate the level of concern that you experience for each of the people (or groups of people) on your second list. Again, 1 equals no concern and 10 equals extreme concern for their welfare. Once again, how much concern do you feel about their welfare?

Finally, list ten people or groups of people you have had no interaction with but you hear about in the news. These individuals or groups might include various people who are struggling with some significant problem. For example, you might consider homeless people on the streets of America, starving people in sections of Africa, women in Afghanistan who suffered under the Taliban, the family of an abducted child you read about in the newspaper, victims of a recent flood or earthquake, and so forth. Again, use the same scale of 1 to 10 to rate the level of concern you experience for each of these people or groups of people on your list. Be honest with yourself about your ratings.

Now, average the scores for each of your three lists above. Add the scores from the first list and divide by ten. Do the same for the other two lists. What is the average number for each of the three lists?

What have you learned from this exercise? How concerned are you for the important people in your life versus the various people you interact with versus strangers in need around the globe? Do you tend to experience similar levels of concern for all people or only for those who you know and love? How much more concerned are you for those your love compared with those you don't even know?

Contemporary Issues with Lack of Concern

Sadly, there are too many examples of members of society showing a total lack of concern for the welfare of others. There are too many examples of people even celebrating the misfortunes of others. This is not a new problem. There are many examples throughout the centuries of people failing to feel and express concern for the struggles of others. People have been cruel and brutal to each other. Slavery, the Holocaust, the more recent genocide in Bosnia and Rwanda, the Crusades during the Middle Ages, and the brutality of the Roman Empire are just a few of the countless examples of people demonstrating a lack of concern for the welfare of others. These examples are dramatic. What are some contemporary and less dramatic examples of lack of concern that you're more likely to be able to relate to? We likely witness or experience the evidence of lack of concern in our daily lives. Here are a few contemporary examples.

Choice of Career and Job Direction

Many people are motivated to choose careers that will make them rich and powerful. They seek money, power, and status. This was especially evident during the middle to late 1990s when the dot-com technology frenzy was at full throttle. In the heart of Silicon Valley and elsewhere, young people fresh out of college were becoming rich overnight with start-up companies and stock options. It seemed like everyone wanted to be part of the action. Curiously, almost all of the advertisements for the January 2000 Super Bowl game were from high tech dot-com companies.

The temptation of fame and fortune minimized the number of students interested in community service and non-profit related careers during these times. Furthermore, few of the companies that were so popular during those years were engaged in trying to make the world or even their communities a better place for those in need. While it was estimated that there were very large numbers of multi-millionaires and even billionaires living and working in the Silicon Valley area, non-profit and community-based service organizations that help those in need were closing their doors due to lack of financial support. Where was the concern for others? How could those with so much not help those with so little?

After the stock market collapsed starting in March 2000, many now unemployed professionals who had a great deal of trouble finding work reassessed their goals and priorities in life. Some turned to the non-profit section and got involved with organizations that try to use their concern for the welfare of others to make the world or their community a better place. Agencies that service the poor and marginalized began to get more applications for volunteers and employees. Yet even with more attention and support, many of these organizations still struggle to stay open.

EXERCISE 7.2

What do you do for work? Does your job or career make the world a better place? Is your job or career a way for you to express your concern for others? If not, could it be? Should it be?

Think about other activities that you engage in. Do you volunteer to help others? Do you give money to help others in need?

List the ways, if any, that your concern for others is expressed through your work, volunteerism, or charitable activities?

Concern for Others in Freeway Accidents

If you spend any time in the car and on freeways, you have likely witnessed traffic accidents. Many are fender benders where no one was hurt. However, too many accidents are severe enough to hurt passengers or even kill them. Inevitably, passing motorists slow down and watch the accident scene as they pass by. This rubber necking can also contribute to accidents.

There have been many reports of people being hurt or even killed on the freeway and nobody stopped to help. A recent fatal accident in the San Francisco Bay Area reportedly had fatalities partially due to the fact that passing motorists did nothing. By the time the paramedics arrived, it was too late. Of course, to be fair, we also hear about heroic behavior on the part of passing motorists who do stop and assist others in distress. However, we also hear too often of other accidents where no one offered to help. Seeing someone in distress on the freeway may elicit concern in passing motorists, but will it also elicit actual behavior to help a stranger in need?

Motorists who have cell phones may call 911 when they witness an accident. However, how many actually stop and offer immediate help.

EXERCISE 7.3

Try and remember times when you passed car accidents on the freeway. Have you seen accidents in which it appeared that people were injured? If so, what did you do? Did you offer help in some way? On a scale of 1 to 10, in which 1 equals no concern and 10 equals a great deal of concern, how concerned were you about the welfare of the injured? Be honest.

What has this brief exercise taught you? How concerned are you for the welfare of injured motorists? How likely are you to try and help a stranger on the freeway?

The point of this and other exercises and examples in this section isn't to make you feel guilty. The point is to help you get a feel for your level of concern when strangers are in trouble and the likelihood that your concern will translate into actual helping actions.

The Gap between Rich and Poor

There have been many news reports about the widening divide between rich and poor Americans. Approximately 25 percent of all children in the United States live below the poverty line (U.S. Census Bureau 2001). About 25 percent of the world's population lives on less than a dollar a day (World Bank 2001). These are striking statistics since so many Americans have much more than they need. So many Americans can afford to buy numerous luxury items, including expensive vacations, electronic devices, cars, and fancy coffee drinks, on a regular basis. Poverty is especially noticeable in many American cities where homeless people beg for money on the street. The contrast between many wealthy residents or workers and the homeless is striking. This is especially true for the wealthy financial and residential sections of many cities. In most major cities in America, you'll see at least one and often several homeless men and women begging on every street corner. It's a striking contrast to see wealthy workers in the financial district of the city and the homeless together on the street. While there's no easy answer to the homeless problem in America, the gap between rich and poor and the lack of concern expressed by many about this division is striking.

How about you? How well off are you? How do you spend your nonessential dollars? How do you feel when you see people who are poor in your location? How concerned are you for their welfare? What if anything do you do about your concern for the poor? Again, the point isn't to instill guilt. The point is to assess your level of concern and the likelihood that you'll act on your concern to assist others less fortunate than yourself.

What we do with our careers and jobs, how we react to people in need, how we balance our greed and self-interest with the needs of others, and how we protect the environment are all contemporary examples of how we are ethically challenged. There are many more examples where our concern for others is tested on a daily basis. The next question is what might be our ethical obligation to express at least a minimal amount of concern for others in our daily lives.

Expressing a Minimal Level of Concern

It would be unrealistic and perhaps ludicrous to think that our concern for others and the environment would result in a full-time commitment to solve all of the world's problems. There's only so much any one person can accomplish. People who have a great deal of influence, talent, and resources can do a tremendous amount to make the world a better place. Most of us, however, can only do so much, given our limitations, potential influence and resources, and responsibilities. What's the minimal level of concern ethical people should feel and express? This is a very difficult question. Of course, feelings are hard to dictate. You generally feel what you feel. However, regardless of your feelings, you can behave in a manner that expresses concern for others. We generally do have control over our behavior, and so we can work towards attending to the welfare of those we can help.

There are obviously so many problems in the world. So many people suffer from all sorts of problems. Tragically, so many lives are stricken with poverty, oppression, disease, and cruelty. How much concern can you muster for all of these issues and how can you best express your concern?

Principles to Live By

You can't just wish that you had more concern for others and have it magically appear. In some respects you either have it or you don't. However, there are several principles that you can follow to try and nurture concern for others:

1. Empathy

2. Treating others as you wish to be treated

3. Recognizing that what is happening to someone today might happen to you tomorrow.

Empathy

As we discussed earlier, some people feel empathy for others while others don't. We all need a certain amount of distance in order to avoid being overwhelmed by all of the suffering in the world. It would be impossible to live your life if you felt a great deal of empathy for every problem and tragedy you heard about. However, you need at least a moderate amount of empathy for others in order to experience and express concern for the welfare of others. You need at least a moderate amount of empathy to ethically contribute to make the world a better place. An exercise might help you better assess your level of empathy towards others.

EXERCISE 7.4

How empathetic are you? When you hear news stories about various tragedies or when friends, relatives, and coworkers experience difficult times, how empathetic do you generally feel? Make a list of five stories that you heard during the past week from the news or from people you know that focus on terrible things that happened to others. These might include a severe illness, a serious marital conflict, a terrible accident, a natural disaster, sudden unemployment, the death of someone you know or of a pet, or other problems. After each item, use a scale of 1 to 10, where 1 is no empathy and 10 is a great deal of empathy, to rate your level of concern for the people (or animals) for each of these items. Add the five scores and divide by five to get an average empathy score.

What has this exercise taught you? How empathetic are you about the sad stories you hear? Does your empathy score surprise you? Are you more or less empathetic than you thought? How empathetic do you think the people who know you best think you are?

Treating Others As You Wish to Be Treated

As discussed earlier, we're likely to experience more concern for others and act on that concern if we agree with the assumption that others should be treated as we would wish to be treated. If we have empathy for others and we feel that we should treat others as we would wish to be treated, then we're on our way towards being more concerned and expressing concern for others.

Concern and Coping with Loss

Suppose you hear that someone at work has lost someone close through a death. Perhaps a coworker experienced the death of a spouse or partner. Maybe they lost a child or a parent or even a pet that they were especially fond of. What should you do? Most people would likely express sympathy by sending a card or saying something like, "So sorry to hear of your loss . . . is there anything I can do?" Perhaps when we say something like, "Is there anything I can do?" we often hope that they will say, "No." If the shoe were on the other foot and it was you who had experienced the loss, what would you want others to do? Think it over. Imagine losing your spouse, partner, child, parent, sibling, or pet. What would you want others to do for you?

Certainly, part of the answer to this question depends on who the other person might be. You would want and expect more from those who are very close to you than from strangers, coworkers, or acquaintances. Furthermore, what you might want immediately following your loss will also differ from what you might want later. Again, putting yourself in the other person's shoes might help you decide how best to express your concern.

Limits to Treating Others As You Wish to Be Treated

Of course there are many limits to treating others as you would wish to be treated. There are only so many hours in the day and days in the week that you can express concern for others. You have your own life to live as well and you have responsibilities that demand your attention and energy. Furthermore, you want to avoid making promises that you can't deliver on. You may make promises to others in need, out of concern, but then not follow up on those promises when other things in your life distract you. So you must maintain realistic expectations concerning how much you can actually deliver when it comes to treating others as you would wish to be treated.

Recognizing That This Could Be You

Another strategy that might help you feel and express more concern for others is to imagine that you'll experience the same situation in the future. We often think that tragedies won't happen to us. How many times have people said to reporters and others that they never thought that the flood, earthquake, tornado, fire, crime, child abduction, layoff, divorce, and other awful events would ever happen to them? Few think that tragedy will strike them.

One excellent example of this is divorce. Probably no one walks down the aisle on that memorable day thinking that the marriage may very well end in divorce. Yet almost 50 percent of first marriages in the United States end in divorce. Furthermore, 60 percent of second marriages end in divorce while 70 percent of third marriages end in divorce (United Nations Department of Economic and Social Affairs 1999). So, the odds of making a better decision about relationships after a first divorce aren't very good. Yet even with these remarkable statistics, the vast majority of people marry, thinking that divorce happens to others but not to them.

People are unrealistically optimistic. Gambling and lotteries wouldn't be so popular if this weren't true. In order to increase our concern and expression of concern for others, we must be able to envision having the problems experienced by others today.

How Do We Translate Our Concern into Action?

There are several things that you can do to translate your concern for others into action.

1. Volunteer somewhere and somehow.

2. Speak up.

3. Grow where you are planted.

Volunteer Somewhere and Somehow

Nothing helps us to nurture and develop our concern for others better than having some direct experience with the issues and struggles of others. Much research as well as anecdotal evidence indicates that you are likely to develop concern and empathy for others when you can attach individual names, faces, and stories to the actual problem or struggle. For example, talking to a homeless person, an HIV/AIDS victim, a hospice patient, an abused child, and so forth provides a perspective that is impossible to obtain otherwise. Observing firsthand the challenging conditions that people face following a flood, tornado, earthquake, or living in an impoverished environment elicits concern, empathy, and action.

Therefore, if you want to nurture your concern and helping behavior towards others you should consider involvement in some type of regular volunteer activity.

Research demonstrates that regular volunteer activities result in positive mental and physical health outcomes. Research suggests that those who volunteer for about two hours per week are more likely to live longer than those who do not even after statistically controlling for age, gender, health behaviors and so forth (Oman 1999). All of the major religious traditions of the world encourage helping those who are less fortunate. While many people engage in volunteer activities as part of their religious activities, many others do so for humanitarian reasons unrelated to religious beliefs. Many report that they receive more from volunteering than they give.

EXERCISE 7.5

How do you give back? What, if any volunteer activities do you currently participate in? If you don't participate in any regular volunteer activities, list the types of human or environmental problems that you might be interested in. For example, are you interested in issues impacting children, the mentally ill, the elderly, the environment? What issues interest you most? Write them down.

Now, consider doing an Internet search on the topics that interest you for possible organizations that work in that area. Determine if a local chapter is located near you. Get information about how you might be able to get involved in a service activity that fits your interests and schedule.

If you have not volunteered regularly, what factors contribute to your not doing so? Time? Other responsibilities? Lack of interest?

Speak Up

A second way to nurture your concern for others is to speak up. You can tell the various people in your life that you're concerned about their welfare. Many people are often shy about expressing their concern for others. Some are embarrassed. Some feel uncomfortable with emotional intimacy. Some may not know how to express their concern in a socially skilled manner. Some may worry that they'll begin to cry or appear weak in expressing their concern for someone. The odds are very high that sincere expression of concern for others (assuming it isn't done in a judgmental or condescending manner) will be welcomed by others.

Speaking up might also include voting, signing a petition, or volunteering for a cause that is important to you. Speaking up might include commenting in meetings about how others should or shouldn't be treated.

Expressing your concern about the welfare of others helps to nurture and develop this concern and often leads to action. An exercise may help you get a better sense of how you express (or fail to express) your concern for others.

EXERCISE 7.6

Think of a time when you were concerned about the welfare of someone and you kept your concern to yourself. Perhaps you were concerned about someone's alcohol problem or their abusive home situation. Perhaps you were concerned about how a loved one, a neighbor, a boss, or a coworker treated that person. Perhaps you were concerned about someone's health.

Now, write down why you think you remained silent with your concern. What factors contributed to you keeping your concern to yourself? Were you afraid of retaliation? Embarrassment? Social discomfort?

Do you regret your silence? If you had to do it all over again would you have behaved differently? If you were to say something now, what would you say?

What have you learned from this exercise? Are there themes that emerge that contribute to preventing you from speaking up when you are concerned about others? Are you self-conscious? Do you feel you should mind your own business? Do you feel embarrassed? Are you afraid of rejection? Here's another exercise to help you figure out what types of issues concern you most.

EXERCISE 7.7

Think about a situation or event in the news where you felt that someone or a group of people were struggling. Think of a situation that elicited your concern. Perhaps you might think of a natural or man made disaster. Perhaps you might think of someone who was victimized in some way. Perhaps you might think of people who have been treated very poorly or have been oppressed. What did you do to express your concern? Did you discuss it with anyone? Did you try to offer help in some way? Would you do anything differently now?

What has this exercise taught you? What kind of news and information elicits concern in you? Are you especially troubled when children or animals are victimized? Are you especially troubled by certain natural disasters such as floods or tornadoes? Are you especially touched by the problems of the poor and oppressed? What, if anything, do you want to do to express your concern?

Grow Where You Are Planted

There are countless troubles and problems in the world. You certainly cannot personally solve or help to solve even a small fraction of these problems. However, you can decide that you will nurture your concern for others and try to express your concern in actions in your day-to-day life, wherever and whenever you can.

You may have various responsibilities and limitations so that you can't always act on your impulse to help others all the time. For example, you may not be able to stop to help a stranded motorist on your way to pick up your child at daycare. However, when opportunities to express your concern for others emerge and you're able to act on that concern, hopefully you'll do so. An exercise can help you figure out how you can express concern where you are in your life.

EXERCISE 7.8

Given the limitations of your particular living, working, and personal situation, how might you grow where you are planted? How might you act on your concern for others in the particular life situation you find yourself in? List five ways that you might be able to act on your concern for others in your life.

Again, in order for you to make progress in expressing your concern for others, you need to want to do it, have good examples to follow, get information from others, and get help from others of like mind.

Have the Desire

To feel concern and express it in some productive manner, you've got to want to do it. This is likely to be especially difficult if you tend to be pretty self-centered or have trouble feeling empathy for others. This book cannot give you the desire. However, if you're reading this book, you must be interested in living more ethically. Experiencing concern and expressing that concern is a necessary component of living more ethically. How exactly you do this is up to you. There are no simple answers. Hopefully, you have the desire. You might just need some direction for that desire.

Find Examples to Follow

In order to feel and express concern, it helps to have some examples. This is especially true if you feel uncomfortable expressing your feelings or find it difficult turning your concern into words and action. Ideally, you want to observe others who are similar to you and your personal and professional situation. In doing so, you might have a better idea about how people who have similar responsibilities and limitations express concern for others. Think of the people in your life who might act as role models for you.

Get Information from Others

Any new behavior needs corrective feedback to fine-tune the behavior. If you're fairly new at expressing concern for others, you might not do it perfectly the first time. You might need to seek out information from someone who's more experienced or knowledgeable to help guide your efforts. Who can provide you with appropriate information and feedback?

Get Help

You may need help from others in order to help you continue to make improvements. Being around others of like mind offers support, reinforcement, and corrective feedback that is invaluable. Do you have friends, family, coworkers, and others in your life who also would like to live more ethically by being more concerned about others? If so, spend time with them to reinforce and nurture each other in your efforts.

Conclusion

This chapter focused on concern for others. It covered strategies you can use to increase your concern for others and express that concern in actual behaviors that count. Now that the discussion of the five ethical principles is complete, it is time to focus on building ethical muscle. Building ethical muscle is likely to be the most challenging part of this book. The hope is to help you to translate your reading of this self-help book into actual behaviors and to help you make ethical decisions during very challenging circumstances.

Test Yourself

Use what you have learned to make tough ethical decisions.

1. You see a homeless person who is very dirty and grimy slip and fall on ice. All this person's belongings have been scattered. What do you do?

2. You see your nemesis at work stranded on the highway with a flat tire, and it is raining heavily. Do you drive by or stop to help? Why or why not?

3. You are planning to buy a new car. Someone you know is desperate for money. Do you give the money to the person in need, or do you purchase the car?

PART 3

Living the Ethical Life

CHAPTER 8

Building Ethical Muscle

Use it or lose it. You probably have heard this expression. It refers to the need to use your muscles, brain, talents, or skills on a regular basis in order to avoid atrophy. The notion of "use it or lose it" is a very important concept when thinking about what you might do with the information that you've learned in this book. How do you apply what you've read to your day-to-day life? How do you make good ethical decisions on a regular basis, long after you've put this book down? How do you make good ethical decisions when there may be negative consequences or significant costs associated with your decisions? How can you develop and build ethical muscle? These questions will be addressed in this chapter.

This is probably the most important chapter in this book. The previous chapters have set the stage for taking what you have learned about ethics and using it to make challenging life decisions. Certainly, applying what you learn to your daily life is one of the ultimate goals for any self-help book. If you've read this far, then you've hopefully learned a great deal about applied ethics. You've learned about the various approaches you can take to think through ethical issues. You've learned procedures to follow in making ethical decisions. You've read about strategies for supporting your ethical efforts (such as getting feedback and support for your efforts, having models, avoiding defensiveness). You've also read about five major ethical principles (integrity, competence, responsibility, respect, and concern) that can help you filter your thinking and decision making. You've got the necessary information to now begin making solid ethical decisions.

However, having useful information isn't enough to change behavior. Many people know that eating high fat foods, smoking cigarettes, and drinking too much alcohol isn't good for them, yet, they may have trouble changing their behavior in these areas. You need more than just information about ethical decision making in order to make good ethical decisions. You need to go further. You need to develop and build ethical muscle. This is especially challenging when you're faced with temptations to *not* make the right or ethical decision because of perceived or actual costs associated with these decisions. It's certainly easy to do the right thing when it doesn't cost you anything. It's obviously much harder to make good ethical decisions when it might cost you money or a promotion or a pleasurable experience. Just as you need to be physically fit to run a race without a lot of pain or discomfort, you need to be ethically fit in order to make good ethical decisions in your journey through life. This is especially true for those really tough decisions.

There are several basic requirements that are needed in order to build ethical muscle. While these have been mentioned in previous chapters, it's important to highlight a few of the important prerequisites if you're going to have a good chance at building ethical muscle.

Five Prerequisites to Build Ethical Muscle

Before you can be ethically fit, you need to meet certain requirements. You can't hope to be successful working out in the ethics gym unless you are prepared. These prerequisites include the following:

1. You've got to want it.

2. You've got to agree with the concept.

3. You've got to have models.

4. You've got to have feedback.

5. You've got to have support.

You've Got to Want It

First, you've got to want it. You can't hope to make solid ethical decisions unless you're motivated to do so. You must tap into whatever reasons were operating for you when you first started reading this ethics book. Something in you is striving to live a more ethical life. If this weren't true, then you wouldn't be reading this book. Perhaps you're concerned about the lack of ethics displayed in your work or home environment. Perhaps you've had some bad experiences with people in your life behaving in an unethical manner. Perhaps you're concerned about all of the examples of unethical behavior that appear in the news. Whatever the reason may be, you've got at least some motivation and interest to live more ethically. It's important to tap into and nurture that interest, motivation, impulse, and desire in order to have any hope of making good future ethical decisions. This is most especially true when making the right decision may carry significant costs.

Behavior is hard to change. For example, many people want to lose weight but can't find the will power, energy, time, or discipline to make their desire come true. The vast majority of people who attempt to lose weight fail to maintain their weight loss. Motivation is necessary to lose weight, but more is needed. This is true for making ethical decisions as well. So motivation is a critical ingredient, but it isn't the only ingredient. You need more.

You've Got to Agree with the Concept

In addition to wanting to live more ethically, you need to agree with the basic framework that has been used in this book to help you filter your decisions. Remember, there are many different ways to approach ethical decision making. You can use a justice approach, a virtue approach, a utilitarian approach, or any of the other approaches discussed. You can use a combination of approaches or different approaches based on the particular ethical decision you're trying to make. Furthermore, you can tailor your approach to ethical decision making somewhat. For example, the virtue approach can emphasize certain ethical virtues (honesty, compassion, love), depending upon your preferences and values. However, in order to live more ethically, you need to agree with the core concepts discussed in the book. For example, it would be impossible to live ethically if you didn't agree that we should all strive towards acting with integrity, competence, responsibility, respect, and concern. While you may choose to add more principles to the list of five discussed here, it seems difficult if not impossible to live ethically without these five basic principles.

Therefore, in order to live more ethically, you need to agree with the ideas and principles outlined in this book. You need to be on board.

You've Got to Have Models

Research in social psychology has consistently shown that you're more likely to learn and change behavior for the better (or for the worse) if you have role models. This is called observational learning (Bandura 1977). It's important to have at least some models in your life that are good examples of someone living ethically. These models could be famous examples, such as Jesus, Buddha, Martin Luther King, Jr., Jimmy Carter, or others. However, they could also be ordinary people in your life such as a parent, coworker, neighbor, or friend. In fact, research has shown that the more likely you see yourself as similar to your model (similar in terms of age, gender, lifestyle, resources), the more powerful and influential the model will be in terms of your ability to learn and change your own behavior. For example, you might say that it's too hard to behave as Jesus would behave. He was special. However, watching a coworker who's a lot like you in many ways and who makes good ethical decisions might inspire you to make better decisions too. You may reason that "if so and so can do this, then so can I."

You've Got to Have Feedback

It'd be rather difficult to shave your face, apply makeup, or comb your hair without access to a mirror. It would be difficult to shoot baskets on a basketball court if you were blindfolded. In order to change behavior and live more ethically, you need to have feedback. You need to have trusted others point out when you behave ethically or unethically. You need to be able to experience the consequences of your ethical and unethical behavior. In order to live more ethically, you need to find a way to get regular feedback on your ethical (or unethical) decision making.

You Have to Have Support

No man is an island. How can you hope to make good solid ethical decisions on a regular basis by yourself, without any community support? This is especially true for those tough ethical decisions when you've got something (perhaps something really big) to lose for doing the right thing. It's vital that you surround yourself with people of like mind so that you can provide mutual support for each other during your most challenging ethical decision making.

These are the basic requirements for living in an ethical manner. Once you have these prerequisites, then you can move on to the next step in building ethical muscle, which is making the difficult and tough ethical choices. This is where the rubber hits the road. There are several ways to build and develop this ethical muscle, which will be the next focus of discussion.

Ways to Build Ethical Muscle

While there are individual preferences and differences on how to build the ethical muscles you'll need to make really difficult decisions, several important principles are likely to prove useful.

The RRICC Mantra

Every decision you make should consider the five ethical principles discussed in this book. You need to think of RRICC (respect, responsibility, integrity, competence, and concern) as a mantra to guide your everyday decisions. Think of the RRICC acronym as a filter to sift through the various thoughts and decisions that you make. As you are confronted with a decision to behave in a particular way, you must ask yourself the following important questions:

1. How can I be respectful to this person or persons?

2. How can I accept responsibility for my thoughts and behavior?

3. How can I maintain integrity by being honest, just, and fair?

4. Am I competent to do this? If not, how should I best manage this issue?

5. How can I best express my concern for others?

Thinking through your decisions with the RRICC lens will hopefully help you to develop and build ethical muscle.

Perhaps it would be useful to put the RRICC mantra on a Post-it on your mirror, desk calendar, wallet, or some other spot that you view frequently. You might put the five key words of the mantra in several locations to help remind yourself to consider these issues before making decisions. Having regular reminders to think in these terms before making decisions will help you to at least consider these important ethical principles prior to making any decisions.

Do-the-Right-Thing Groups

In order to maximize your ability to build ethical muscle, it's important to surround yourself with people of like mind. The best way to do this is by having regular do-the-right-thing group meetings planned. What's a do-the-right-thing group? You can call it whatever you want. Perhaps you might call it an ethics group or a RRICC group, if you wish. It's simply a group of people of any size that agrees to meet on a regular basis to discuss ethical issues that participants face, so that you can receive the input and support of like-minded people.

Many people today participate in book clubs. In some respects, book clubs can act as both an intellectually stimulating discussion of a book but also can act as a support group. Many people take early morning walks with friends or neighbors for exercise. Most neighborhoods are filled with these walking groups each morning. In addition to physical exercise, these folks often discuss the various things going on in their lives and receive support from others about life decisions, conflicts, and so forth. For many, these walking groups are a combination of physical exercise and group therapy.

If you're really serious about living ethically, it might be useful and productive to join or start some kind of ethics group. Perhaps you know some people who would like to get together once each month or so to discuss ethical dilemmas that they have faced in recent days and weeks. You can then help each other solve ethical dilemmas and support good ethical decisions.

This group approach to ethical decision making has several important advantages. First, it forces group members to think about and consider their behavior and decisions through the lens of ethical decision making on a regular basis. Second, the group provides a number of different people with various perspectives to assist in ethical problem solving. Perhaps ten or fifteen heads thinking through the issues associated with ethical decisions is much better than only one head. Third, regular group meetings can provide the necessary support and encouragement that is needed to make and maintain really tough ethical decisions. Finally, surrounding yourself with people who are trying to live more ethically can be fun. Being with like-minded people can have the emotional advantages of many other kinds of self-help or support groups.

You can make the experience of meeting together pleasant and enjoyable. You can meet over a meal or while exercising if you wish. The key ingredient is for several people to regularly discuss ethical issues in a relaxed and pleasant environment.

How to Conduct a Do-the-Right-Thing Group

Once you've got a group of people who are willing and able to commit to living a more ethical life and who agree to meet regularly to discuss ethical issues, you might want to structure the meetings in a way to maximize the experience for everyone.

First, it's important to ensure that everyone uses the RRICC principles in dealing with each other. In order to work towards living a more ethically sound life, you need to start with how you interact with each other. This might seem obvious but it's still important to attend to and nurture. Therefore, treating others in the group with respect and concern is a must. Furthermore, maintaining integrity, responsibility, and competence is also an important requirement in interacting with each other. If anyone does violate the RRICC principles in interacting with each other, careful corrective feedback would be needed.

Second, you might begin each meeting with the development of an agenda. It helps to come up with a list of topics that individuals want to discuss. Sometimes issues may overlap. The key is to ensure that everyone's issues and concerns are addressed as best as you can. You want to avoid the same person or people getting all the attention all the time. You want to mix the needs of the group members around so that everyone has about the same air time.

Work through the agendas as best as you can, but be sure that the group sessions begin and end on time. It's important to be respectful of each other's time with this commitment to begin and end on time. In this way, people can plan accordingly regarding their other commitments and responsibilities.

Finally, you might want to end the group with a review of the discussion, highlighting the ethical lessons learned during the meeting. You might wish to review the ethical discussion through the RRICC lens as well.

There are no right and wrong ways to run these group meetings. These suggestions are provided to give you some recommendations and guidance. You'll want to adapt the group structure and discussions in a way that meets the needs of your members. The most important thing is that you meet regularly, that you support each other in your efforts to live more ethically, and that it's fun. Face it, if it isn't fun and worthwhile for everyone, then the group will likely not continue over time.

Remember, Rome Wasn't Built in a Day

It's important to keep in mind that in order to build ethical muscle and make tough decisions, you'll make unethical decisions at times. No one is able to make the right call every time. In fact, there may be times when you know what the right decision is but choose not to make it because the costs are too high. You'll need to be patient with yourself. You must keep in mind that it takes time and effort to build ethical muscle. It may be helpful to think of building ethical muscle as a process that involves repeated thinking, problem solving, and decision making that's never perfect.

This is an important principle. In order to build ethical muscle, you can't be overly discouraged or quit trying when you fail to meet your expectations for change. These things take time. A particular failure doesn't mean that you can't build muscle over time.

Furthermore, any efforts in the right direction are better then nothing. Thinking about ethical issues more seriously and carefully, using the RRICC model, discussing these concerns with friends and others of like mind: all are better then doing nothing. Even if you consciously choose to not do the right thing because you can't handle the consequences, thinking through ethical challenges and recognizing them in places where you didn't before you read this book is a big step in the right direction.

Maintain Continuous Assessment

In order to build ethical muscle you must continue to evaluate yourself and your decision making regularly. You must find a way to constantly evaluate your decisions and determine what you might or might not do differently in the future. How can you accomplish this? Certainly, by participating in a support group, you can have the group members help you with regular assessment. You can also, if you wish, maintain an ethics journal where you can keep track of the ethical decisions that you make. There are many different ways that you can maintain continuous assessment. You just want to be sure that you do, in fact, constantly evaluate your decision making and progress.

EXERCISE 8.1

What do you now need to do to build ethical muscle? List at least five things you need to do in order to help yourself make better ethical decisions. Who do you need to consult with? What do you need to read? How might you alter your lifestyle? What can you realistically do to build ethical muscle for those really tough ethical dilemmas and situations ahead of you? What is your plan of action?

Tough Ethical Decisions

As you begin to feel more at ease thinking about day-to-day decisions as ethical decisions and get used to living ethically each day, then you will be much better prepared when you come across a really tough ethical dilemma. You will have built ethical muscle and you'll be ready for the challenge of a really hard ethical dilemma. It's impossible to know exactly what kind of really tough ethical decisions you will have to make in your life. The following examples—including marital affairs, participating in unethical practices at work, and spending money on yourself rather than others—will hopefully give you a flavor for some of the tough ethical decisions that are quite common.

Marital Affairs

Marital infidelity is certainly an ethical issue. On the surface, you might immediately think that marital infidelity is always unethical. However, different ethical approaches may result in different ways of thinking about infidelity through an ethics lens.

For example, the absolute moral rule approach might suggest that marital infidelity is always wrong and thus unethical. However, the utilitarian approach might suggest that it isn't unethical if most of the people involved would be happier if the marital infidelity occurred. The egoism approach might also suggest that marital infidelity is okay as long as you feel comfortable and justified in the behavior. The cultural relativism approach might suggest that ethnic, cultural, religious, and other factors must be considered before deciding if marital infidelity is ethical or not. In some subcultures, affairs might be justified while in some other subcultures, they are not.

There are many marital circumstances that might make a discussion of the ethics of marital infidelity very complicated. For example, suppose that you were married to someone who is extremely physically and emotionally abusive. Suppose this person also was severely alcoholic and participated in affairs regularly. Perhaps this spouse abandoned you and your children, disappearing for months and years at a time. While technically not divorced, you might feel divorced. You might feel more ethically justified in having an affair under these conditions.

In another scenario, suppose your spouse became severely disabled in an accident or from a serious chronic illness. Suppose the disability resulted in an inability to have sexual or other interpersonal relations. Suppose your loving spouse encouraged you to have an affair to fulfill some of your sexual and emotional needs. Or perhaps your spouse was in a coma and was now living on life support. Suppose there was no chance that your spouse could become conscious again. Again, you might feel more justified having an affair under these circumstances. These examples make clear that all of the facts of a particular ethical dilemma must be considered before a thoughtful decision can be made. All marital affairs are not the same.

Thinking about the possibility of participating in an affair should not only include an analysis of the facts but also the various approaches to ethics. Thinking about the potential affair through the lens of the RRICC mantra is also necessary. Here's how you might look at a potential affair using the five ethical principles highlighted in this book.

Respect. How might having an affair respect the rights, dignity, and feelings of someone else? Depending upon the circumstances of the potential affair, you might be disrespectful to the rights of several others (your spouse, the other person's spouse, your children, the children of the other person). However, your potential affair might not result in disrespectful behavior if, for example, your spouse was disabled and wanted you to have other relationships, given his or her medical situation.

Responsibility. How might the potential affair impact your responsibility for your thoughts and actions? You might behave in a highly irresponsible manner by avoiding obligations to your family and work. You might become so preoccupied with managing the affair that you would neglect your various roles, obligations, and promises to others. Once confronted about your affair, you might not take responsibility for your actions, instead blaming the affair on the behaviors of others (saying that your spouse drove you into the arms of another).

Integrity. How honest, fair, and just could you be during a marital affair? Many affairs are associated with consistent lying. Many affairs are managed through deceit. How dishonest would you be by having an affair? Are you being fair to relevant parties (spouse and children)? Once found out, would people who are important to you trust you again?

Competence. Many people who have affairs neglect their work and other obligations. Perhaps they're so focused on their relationship that they no longer act in a competent manner at work or at home. Perhaps they don't drive competently because they're distracted.

How would a potential affair impact your competence as a spouse, parent, worker, driver, and so forth?

Concern. How might having an affair impact your concern for others? How would it impact your other relationships and the feelings of others, such as spouses and children? Might the excitement, pleasure, and work to manage the affair make you more insensitive to the needs and wishes of others?

After considering the different ethical approaches to the question of having a marital affair and evaluating the situation using the RRICC model, it would be important to discuss the situation with trusted others. Perhaps you would include this issue in a do-the-right-thing group meeting. If you weren't comfortable talking about a potential or actual marital affair with a group of other people, you might identify someone you trust whom you could discuss the issue with.

After going through these steps, you'd be ready to make a decision. Whatever that decision might be, you'd want to reconsider your decision in retrospect in order to learn from the experience for future decisions.

It's certainly possible that feeling passion for another would alter your critical thinking abilities. It you feel drawn to someone due to passion and chemistry, it might be very difficult to make a good decision. Taking a few breaths and going through the process discussed above might at least increase the odds that a good decision will be made. While there are no guarantees that using the ethical decision-making approach will always result in the right decision, it at least increases the chances of your considering the ethical implications of this challenging and fairly common tough ethical dilemma.

Unethical Practices at Work

You might be forced to participate in what you consider to be many unethical behaviors at your workplace. Perhaps you work in the food industry and serve or deliver food that you wouldn't eat yourself. Maybe you're instructed to lie to clients or deceive others on direct orders from your boss. Perhaps you work in an industry that makes products that you feel are harmful and maybe deadly to others. Here are a few examples to give you a feel for really challenging ethical dilemmas at work.

Tim's Story

Tim works as a bartender at an upscale restaurant. He serves alcohol to hundreds of people each day in this trendy spot. Over time, he gets to know many of his regular customers. After drinking, many confide in him about their personal problems and conflicts including marital infidelity, work problems, and so forth. He doesn't want to know all of the information he hears and doesn't know what to do with the information once he gets it. Furthermore, he learns that a number of his clients have alcohol-related problems and drink too much. They then drive off and are at risk of getting into a serious car accident. Tim feels that he, by the nature of his job, participates in their alcohol and personal problems. He enjoys being a bartender but feels that he's being asked to participate in challenging ethical dilemmas. He dreads the day when one of his customers will get into a tragic car accident after he has served him or her alcohol. He dreads the day when a customer's spouse will come in, because he knows about his customer's marital infidelities. He wonders if the guy who drank too much at the restaurant will get himself home safely. He feels that it is extremely hard to refuse to serve more alcohol to a drunken customer when that customer happens to be the city police chief, the mayor, or the local congressman.

Carol's Story

Carol works as a pastry chef at a fancy and expensive restaurant. She sees all sorts of curious behavior at the restaurant. For example, she witnesses coworkers not handling food in a sanitary manner and food being served that is marginal to eat. She feels that although she works hard to always do the right thing at work, the executive chef insists that she uses products that might be stale or not edible in some way. She feels that if she were to say anything she'd lose her job. When she discusses her concerns with friends at other restaurants, they usually say that it's that way there as well. They claim that she's too idealistic and that the whole industry is corrupt in this way. They usually say, "Hey, if you can't take the heat in the kitchen, then get out." However, she feels that she's an excellent pastry chef and doesn't really want to start a new career. Furthermore, she needs her salary to support herself and a disabled husband.

Robert's Story

Robert works as a stockbroker. He advises all sorts of people on stock purchases and other financial matters. His company frequently encourages him and the other employees to push the sale of certain stocks because the investment firm makes generous profits from the sale of these financial products. He's encouraged to push these stocks to vulnerable clients who know little about stock purchases since they'll ask few questions and trust the advice given by the company. He feels that if he's honest with his advice, then he'll lose his job as well. Since he enjoys being a stockbroker and he has opportunities for advancement, he doesn't want to rock the boat. Furthermore, he has a new baby at home and his wife wants to stop working so that she can spend more time being a parent. Being out of a job now would cause a tremendous hardship on his wife and child.

Carlos's Story

Carlos works for a defense contractor building various weapons for the military. He's an engineer and is an excellent employee for the company. He notices that his boss and other top executives cut corners in a number of ways in order to save money and earn bigger profits. Carlos thinks that these cost-cutting strategies may severely compromise the effectiveness of some of the products the company makes. He fears the possibility that a weapon system, military aircraft, or other products may not adequately work in the field, which could result in the death of many soldiers. When he tactfully mentions his concerns to his boss, he's told to mind his own business. Carlos loves his work but feels that if he says anything else he'll lose his job and might become a scapegoat. He feels that his silence contributes to the problem and could easily result in people being harmed or killed if the military equipment is faulty.

These examples provide a flavor for the types of ethical challenges people may face at work. Doing the right thing in all of these cases could result in the loss of a job or career. Losing a job or career might also have other important implications for family members and others. How would you manage these tough decisions?

While there are no easy answers to these dilemmas, following the principles discussed in the book will hopefully help you make better decisions even when your ethical conflicts are really challenging.

First, get all of the relevant facts regarding your dilemma. Then, you'll want to think about the various ethical approaches to your ethical issue. How might the utilitarian, common good, justice, egoism, and others approaches help you think through the various issues? How might our RRICC approach enlighten you? How can you be respectful, maintain responsibility for your actions, maintain personal integrity, maintain competence, and express concern for others? Perhaps you can then discuss the dilemma with your group or trusted others. Can you live with the consequences of losing your job or career if that's what the likely outcome might be if you do the right thing? Can you live with the implications of doing the right thing? Can you live with the implications of *not* doing the right thing if a death or severe harm could have been avoided if you spoke up? Finally, make a decision and then consider it in retrospect.

Spending Money on Yourself Rather Than Others

Most of us would love to have more money to spend on our needs, hobbies, vacations, and various adult toys, such as nice cars, boats, clothes, and electronic equipment. We all must find strategies for managing our money. Most of us don't have unlimited resources and thus are confronted with the often challenging ethical dilemma of making hard choices about how to spend our money. For example, if you buy the vacation home, then you can't save much for your children's education. If you buy the expensive espresso drinks each morning on your way to work, then you can't give money to the homeless shelter. If you buy the expensive home, then you can't afford to care for your elderly parent. How much are we willing to sacrifice our needs and desires for the needs and desires of important others. How do we manage our limited resources given our needs and desires and those of various other people? These questions can often result in very challenging and tough ethical dilemmas.

Here's a few examples of financial challenges that result in tough ethical dilemmas.

Hector's Story

Hector and his wife have just saved enough money to finally buy their own home in a nice neighborhood. They are pleased that they finally will have adequate room to live and the children will finally be able to attend a quality school. Furthermore, the new house will provide enough room to allow them to think about having another child. Hector's mother suddenly develops a serious illness and has very little financial resources since her husband died a few years ago and they had little savings. Hector is an only child and so he doesn't have brothers and sisters that can help his mother. His mother's illness requires expensive treatment and rehabilitation, and insurance won't pay for much of these expenses. Hector considers not buying the home they were planning on buying in order to have money to help his mother. Not buying the home will result in his children staying in a marginal school and living in a rather unsafe neighborhood.

Bob's Story

Bob has a gambling problem. He gets into debt and has borrowed money from unsavory characters. His gambling problems have been chronic and all treatment efforts have failed. Bob is now in some real trouble and needs to pay off a bookie over $50,000 in gambling debts. He could be severely hurt or even killed if he doesn't pay the debt. He comes to his mother for help. She's a disabled and elderly woman who is recovering from hip replacement surgery. She has limited financial resources as well, and helping her son would wipe out all of her savings. Her other children feel strongly that helping Bob again would not change him. He has drained everyone he knows of money over the years, and few people are willing to help him now, no matter how desperate he becomes. They claim that even if he gets out of trouble today, he'll get in more trouble tomorrow. What does his mother do?

Kim and Jose's Story

Kim and Jose saved money, worked very hard, and have made many sacrifices over the years to help their daughter, Angelica, get a good education and save for college. During Angelica's first year in college, she gets involved with a service group that provides food and shelter to the homeless in her community. After several months, Angelica feels so touched by the struggles of the homeless that she wants to drop out of school and give her college savings to the homeless shelter. She reasons that her education is a luxury and that food and shelter for others is a necessity. She believes that the shelter can use the money better than she can. What do Kim and Jose do?

In all of these and similar examples you would want to follow the ethical decision-making procedures outlined in the book to help you decide what the best course of action would be. Again, you would want to start by getting all of the relevant facts together. Then, you would want to consider how the various ethical approaches might guide you. Then, you could use the RRICC model to consider what course of action would be respectful to others and maintain your responsibility for your behavior, as well as your integrity. You would also want to consider how your actions might impact your competence and concern for the relevant parties. Your next step would be to discuss the dilemma with your do-the-right-thing group or a trusted other. Finally, you should make a decision and consider it in retrospect.

It's important to mention once again that following the guidelines presented here might not result in a crystal clear decision. The tougher the issue, the harder it will be to come up with a decision that will be easy and straightforward. You may be unable to come up with a clear path to follow. However, the process will hopefully help you better think through really challenging ethical dilemmas and maximize the odds that the decisions you do make will be solid ethical decisions.

EXERCISE 8.2

Think about the reasons that you decided to read this book. What issues or ethical questions or dilemmas emerged that contributed to you seeking out ethical guidance through the reading of this book? Perhaps you've had or are about to face a really tough ethical dilemma. What is it? If you don't know for sure, then what are some of the most likely challenging ethical dilemmas you'll face in the foreseeable future? Do you have something clear in your mind? Once you have something in mind, answer the following questions:

1. What are the facts of the ethical dilemma?

2. What are the different options you can choose?

3. How might different approaches to ethics guide you in your decision making?

4. Of the approaches that sit best with you (egoism, utilitarianism, common good, and so on) which approach or approaches do you find most relevant to the situation, and how might they guide you?

5. Use the RRICC model to consider your dilemma. What is the role or impact of respect, responsibility, integrity, competence, and concern on your decision making?

6. Who can you discuss the situation with? What do others suggest you do?

7. Make a decision and act.

8. Consider your decision now in retrospect. What worked well? What worked poorly? What would you do in the future if you found yourself with the same dilemma?

9. Use this process and model for other big ethical dilemmas in your life.

Conclusion

This chapter focused on building ethical muscles to make really tough ethical decisions. It also stressed the importance of using the RRICC mantra, participating in do-the-right-thing groups, and remembering that continuous assessment and ethical working out is needed to build ethical muscle and make solid ethical decisions. Finally, it looked at several common themes that are frequently associated with really tough ethical dilemmas.

Test Yourself

Use what you have learned to make tough ethical decisions.

1. You find out that your child cheated on his or her college entrance exams. Your child was admitted to a very competitive college based at least in part on the entrance exam results. What do you do? Why?

2. You were laid off and are now desperately looking for work. You are offered a good job and agree that you will commit to the job for a year. Three months later, you are offered a far superior job at another company. Do you take the new job? Why or why not?

3. You are a medical doctor, and a pharmaceutical company offers you an all-expenses-paid trip to an exotic location. In accepting the trip, it is expected that you'll promote their drugs in your medical practice. This may not be in the best interest of your clients or your company. Your spouse really wants to go on this trip. What do you do?

CHAPTER 9

Now What?

You've now come to the end of the book. Hopefully, you've got a much clearer picture of ways to observe, evaluate, and make solid ethical decisions. You should now have much more sensitivity to the ethical issues and dilemmas in daily life and have some useful and productive strategies for making really tough ethical decisions. You've got the tools to make solid ethical decisions both now and in the future. Now what?

It's one thing to carefully read a self-help book and learn something from it. It's an entirely different matter to take what you've learned and apply it to your life after you put the book down. What can you do to maximize the chances that this experience will ultimately help you in your life and in your decision making? Where do you go from here? What are some of the likely obstacles along your way? Where can you get further help if you need it?

This chapter will address these questions and more.

Five Precautions on Living More Ethically

There are a variety of pitfalls likely to emerge for those interested in living more ethically. It is important to be aware of these in order to avoid them as you move forward.

1. *Avoiding Ridgity*

Many people who are interested in ethics and who attempt to follow ethical principles risk becoming rigid. Some may consider ethical dilemmas in an all-or-nothing manner. It's important to reiterate that ethical decision making can often create more questions than answers to problems and dilemmas. Someone who's focused on doing the right thing can be tempted to develop rigid ways of thinking and behaving. Again, we must practice what we preach using our RRICC mantra in all areas of our life. Rigid thinking can ultimately result in being disrespectful and showing a lack concern for the opinions and perspectives of others. Hopefully, living more ethically means being more humble and not becoming a know-it-all. Someone who is always right is hardly ethical. Someone who is always right is hard to be around, as well.

2. *Avoiding Arrogance*

Many who are focused on living more ethically might be at risk for becoming arrogant. They may feel that they're one of the few people around who know what to do in various situations. They may develop the idea that they alone adequately understand what the right thing is regarding any number of challenging situations. This arrogance again violates the RRICC principle of being respectful and showing concern for others. Again, humility is one of the more likely outcomes of a sincere effort to live more ethically. Being arrogant isn't being respectful and demonstrating concern for others. Furthermore, it isn't fun or pleasant to be around someone who is arrogant.

3. *Avoiding Indecision*

Another risk you may encounter in trying to live more ethically is indecision. If you really consider all of the ethical implications of your various decisions, you can potentially feel paralyzed by indecision because there are so many different ways to approach an ethical dilemma. Obviously, you must live your life and make all sorts of quick decisions on a daily basis. Perhaps reading this book has made you more sensitive to the ethical implications of your daily decisions. Perhaps it has given you a model to think through these decisions better. Careful and thoughtful ethical analysis is important, but you must also be careful to avoid indecisiveness as you try to use what you've learned. You must remember that there is no guarantee that you will always make the best ethical choice. However, if you use the tools provided in this book and you are sensitive to the ethical implications of your decisions, you'll likely make many more right calls than wrong ones.

4. Avoiding Atrophy

Behavior is always hard to change. That's a given. If you're going to try to live more ethically using the procedures and models discussed in this book, you'll need to find a way to avoid ethical atrophy. Good intentions and motivation, as mentioned many times in this book, will only take you so far in your efforts to change the way you go about making ethical decisions. Just as you need to continuously work out to maintain physical fitness, you'll need to regularly work out to maintain ethical fitness. This is why the notion of a do-the-right-thing group and following the RRICC mantra is so important. You might consider other strategies, as well, that are unique to your needs and your living or work situation, to help avoid ethical atrophy in the coming weeks, months, and years.

5. Avoiding Being a Doormat

Your efforts to live more ethically might put you at some risk for being a doormat. In other words, if you are a goody-goody always trying to do the right thing, people may try to take advantage of you. Your efforts to be concerned for the needs of others, to be honest and fair, and to be fully responsible for your thoughts and actions may all make you a target for others who choose to live their lives with minimal ethics. You may wish to be sensitive to this issue (without being paranoid) and try to minimize situations and circumstances where others can take advantage of your efforts to live more ethically.

Four Obstacles to Living More Ethically

It is easy to give up on living more ethically. It can be hard work with perhaps little obvious payoff at times. Here are several common obstacles that may be ahead of you.

1. The Costs Are Too Big

The biggest obstacle to living more ethically has to be the costs of doing so. What are the cost implications for living more ethically?

Can you afford these costs? Might it mean that you lose some friendships or your job or money or pleasures that you have come to
value?

It's so much easier to live ethically when it costs you nothing
than when it costs you a lot. Making tough ethical decisions will
likely have some consequences that could hurt you or those you care
about. It certainly won't feel good to have important people in your
life angry or upset with you. It certainly won't feel good to be honest
about your limitations. It can't feel good to write out an extra big
check to the IRS. It can't feel good to pass over a great opportunity
for pleasure, advancement, or monetary gains. Doing the right thing
can hurt you. It can sting. You'll have to ask yourself if doing the
right thing in a really tough ethical dilemma is worth it to you.

This book has outlined ways to try and make a commitment to
live more ethically. However, as you face each of the ethical dilemmas in your life, to some degree you'll need to do a cost-benefit analysis to determine if the benefits outweigh the costs or if the costs
outweigh the benefits. You certainly may be tempted to make unethical decisions, given the costs of doing the right thing. It would be
hard to get through life without some of these temptations. How you
handle these temptations and impulses to behave unethically is
another matter. Having a well-thought-out game plan is critical to
help you make tough ethical decisions when they emerge.

2. Lack of a Game Plan

It's foolish to think that you can significantly alter your behavior if you don't have a game plan. Many people try to find a mate,
lose weight, improve their physical fitness, and so forth without any
organized plan about achieving their goals. This is also true regarding living more ethically. It's not reasonable to think that you can
live more ethically solely by willing it. You need a plan of attack. In
fact, you'll need a really good plan of attack especially for those
really hard ethical decisions. This book has tried to help you develop
a game plan by discussing the RRICC mantra, ways of thinking
through ethical dilemmas, encouraging you to get support from
others for your efforts, and so forth. However, you'll need to tweak
these guidelines to fit your needs, personality, living situation, and
work environment.

You need to have a specific plan about how you're going to
best handle ethical dilemmas as they emerge. This is especially true
for those really tough decisions when the temptation will be very
high to not do the right thing. Thinking that you'll make good ethical
decisions (especially those tough decisions) in the moment when

they occur and with lots of temptations to behave unethically is likely to result in failure. So, given all that you've learned by reading this book and completing the various exercises within, what's your game plan to live more ethically? Is your game plan realistic?

3. Unrealistic Expectations

After reading this a self-help book, you may be feeling especially enthusiastic and excited about working on ethical dilemmas. While this enthusiasm is great, be careful to keep your expectations for change realistic. You might be fired up to live a more ethical life and have wonderful intentions. However, the reality is that you may not always make good ethical choices every time you are confronted with an ethical dilemma. This is especially true when you're facing a really tough ethical dilemma. If you maintain realistic expectations, you'll hopefully not be overly disappointed when you fail to live up to your ideal. You'll be less likely to give up. You'll pick your self up after a failure or a disappointment and start all over again.

4. Lack of Help

Living more ethically is challenging enough. Doing it alone, without any help from others, it's nearly impossible. Again, help can be obtained from a number of resources, including people who are trying to live more ethically just like you. This could include family, friends, or members of a do-the-right-thing group. Help can be provided in other ways as well. Perhaps additional reading or reviewing relevant Web sites might be useful to you. Perhaps getting involved with church or civic organizations might be valuable to you as well. Maybe you would find it useful to take an appropriate course on ethics. You may want to take a look at the resources section at the end of this book.

Three Next Steps

Now that you've briefly examined some of the major precautions and obstacles to living more ethically, what will you do next? Your immediate next steps should be to commit yourself to living more ethically; to use the RRICC model, the five-step decision-making process, and the various approaches to ethics in your daily life, for both small and big ethical decisions; and to get involved with others of like mind.

1. Commit Yourself

Just by reading this book, you've made some commitment to at least learn more about ethical decision making. Now you're asked to take that initial interest and turn it into action. Thus, you're now asked to commit yourself to be more sensitive to ethical issues and dilemmas and to use the tools provided to you in this book to make good solid ethical decisions in all of your life decisions. What do you need to do now to fully commit yourself to this effort? How can you turn your interest into action?

2. Use the Tools

After making a commitment to live more ethically, you need to use the tools provided to you in this book to increase the odds that your commitment to living more ethically has some useful and productive structure to it. The tools of the RRICC mantra, the five-step process for ethical decision making, the various approaches to ethics, and so forth are all designed to help you turn your commitment into sustainable action. So use the tools. Do whatever you need to do to remind yourself to use the tools on a daily basis.

3. Don't Do It Alone

Finally, you need to have help with your efforts. Do-the-right-thing groups or more informal efforts to get support and guidance will help you. This is especially true when it comes to really tough ethical dilemmas. Find someone or a group of people to work with on living more ethically. Don't do it alone.

Conclusion

Good luck and best wishes in your efforts to live more ethically. The fact that you've read this book demonstrates that you've got some important interest in this topic and you desire a more ethical life for yourself and those around you. This is a big step in your effort to live more ethically. Now you need to take it on the road and turn your interest into action. Hopefully in doing so you'll live a more satisfying life and make the world a better place for both yourself and others. Helping to create a more humane and just world is a noble and worthwhile goal. This is true even if you do so only in the little corner of the globe where you live, work, and play. So, in the words of my grandfather, "Always do the right thing." I think that you (as well as others in your life) will ultimately be glad you did.

Resources

If you are interested in additional materials to read, there are a number of books, Web sites, and other resources that you can use to help you in your efforts to live more ethically. This is hardly an exhaustive list, but it highlights some resources that you might find of value.

Recommended Books

All of the books listed are written for lay readers and are fairly practical in orientation.

A Question of Values: Six Ways We Make the Personal Choices That Shape Our Lives, by Hunter Lewis. Crozet, Va.: Axios Press, 2000.

How Good People Make Tough Choices: Resolving the Dilemmas of Ethical Living, by Rushworth M. Kidder. New York: Simon and Schuster, 1995.

Integrity, by Stephen L. Carter. New York: HarperCollins, 1996.

What Matters Most: The Power of Living Your Values, by Hyrum W. Smith. New York: Simon and Schuster, 2000.

Making Choices: Practical Wisdom for Everyday Moral Decisions, by Peter Kreeft. Ann Arbor, Mich.: Servant Publications, 1990.

Good Work: When Excellence and Ethics Meet, by Howard Gardner, Mihaly Csikszentmihalyi, and William Damon. New York: Basic Books, 2001.

A Crisis of Spirit: Our Desperate Search for Integrity, by Anita L. Spencer. New York: Plenum Press, 1996.

Moral Wisdom and Good Lives, by John Kekes. Ithaca, N.Y.: Cornell University Press, 1995.

Everyday Ethics: Inspired Solutions to Real-Life Dilemmas, by Joshua Halberstam. New York: Penguin Books, 1993.

Writings on an Ethical Life, by Peter Singer Peter. New York: Ecco Press, 2001.

Practical Ethics, by Peter Singer. New York: Cambridge University Press, 1993.

Beyond Bumper Sticker Ethics: An Introduction to Theories of Right and Wrong, by Steven Wilkens. Westmont, Ill.: Intervarsity Press, 1995.

Recommended Web Sites

www.scu.edu/ethics/
> The Markkula Center for Applied Ethics at Santa Clara University offers a variety of articles, Web links, and other information about applied ethics.

commfaculty.fullerton.edu/lester/ethics/general.html
> The School of Communications at California State University, Fullerton, offers this helpful Web site with numerous links to ethics on the Web in many categories.

www.ethics.org.au/
> The St. James Ethics Centre is a nonprofit organization that promotes ethics in daily life. It is not associated with any religious or political affiliations.

www.ethics.ubc.ca/resources/
> This site offers useful links to a variety of applied ethic topics.

www.globalethics.org
> The Institute for Global Ethics is an independent, nonprofit, nonsectarian, and nonpartisan organization that promotes ethics globally.

Other Resources

You might want to contact your local library, university, church, or other civic organizations to see what ethical decision-making resources might be available to you in your community. There may be groups, programs, and other opportunities to learn and grow regarding applied ethics in your community.

References

American Psychological Association. APA. 1992. Ethical principles of psychologists and code of conduct. *American Psychologist* 47: 1597-1611.

Bandura, A. 1977. *Social Learning Theory*. Englewood Cliffs, N.J.: Prentice-Hall.

Boy Scouts of America. 2002. Boy Scout Oath, Law, Motto, and Slogan.Scouting.org. Retrieved September 18, 2002 from the World Wide Web: http://www.scouting.org/factsheets// 02-503a.html

Bushman, B. 2002. Does venting anger feed or extinguish the flame? *Personality and Social Psychology Bulletin* 28:724-731.

Ethics Officer Association. American Society of Chartered Life Underwriters and Chartered Financial Consultants. 1997. *Sources and Consequences of Workplace Pressure: Increasing the Risk of Unethical Business Practices*. Waltham, MA: Author.

Kruger, J., and D. A. Dunning. 1999. Unskilled and unaware of it: How difficulties in recognizing one's own incompetence lead to inflated self-assessments. *Journal of Personality and Social Psychology* 77:1121-1134.

Kuschel, K. J., and H. Haring. 1993. *Hans Kung: New Horizons for Faith and Thought*. London: SCM Press Ltd.

Luskin, F. 2002. *Forgive for Good: A Proven Prescription for Health and Happiness*. San Francisco: Harper Collins.

Myers, D. G. 2000. The funds, friends, and faith of happy people. *American Psychologist* 55:56-67.

Oman, D. 1999. Volunteerism and mortality among the community-dwelling elderly. *Journal of Health Psychology* 4:301-316.

Plante, T. G. (Ed.). 1999. *Bless Me Father for I Have Sinned: Perspectives on Sexual Abuse Committed by Roman Catholic Priests.* Westport, Conn.: Praeger/Greenwood.

———. 2004. *Sin Against the Innocents: Sexual Abuse by Priest and the Role of the Catholic Church.* Westport, Conn.: Praeger/Greenwood.

Rachels, J. 2003. *The Elements of Moral Philosophy.* Fourth edition. New York: McGraw-Hill.

Scheer, R. 1976. Playboy interview: Jimmy Carter-a candid conversation with the Democratic candidate for the presidency. *Playboy,* November, 63-86.

Singer, P. 1999. "The Singer Solution to World Poverty." *The New York Times Magazine,* September, 60-63.

U. S. Census Bureau. 2001. *Poverty in the United States 2001: Current Populations Reports.* Washington, D.C.: U. S. Census.

United Nations Department of Economic and Social Affairs. 1999. *Demographic Yearbook: 1997.* 49th edition. New York: United Nations Department of Economic and Social Affairs.

Wadden, T. A., J. A. Sternberg, K. A. Letizia, A. J. Stunkard, and G. D. Foster. 1989. Treatment of obesity by very low calorie diet, behavior therapy, and their combination: A five-year perspective. *International Journal of Obesity* 13:39-46.

World Bank Group. 2001. *World Bank Report 2000/2001: Attacking Poverty.* Washington, D.C.: World Bank Group.

Thomas G. Plante, Ph.D., ABPP is professor of psychology and director of the Center for Professional Development at Santa Clara University. He is also adjunct clinical associate professor in psychiatry and behavioral sciences at the Stanford University School of Medicine, and consulting associate professor in the Stanford University School of Education. He is a licensed psychologist with a private practice in Menlo Park, CA. For more than a decade, he has taught classes in ethics at both Santa Clara and Stanford universities and conducted workshops in ethics for mental health-care professionals as well as for the public. Plante is the author of *Contemporary Clinical Psychology, Second Edition* (2005, Wiley); editor of *Bless Me Father For I Have Sinned: Perspectives on Sexual Abuse Committed by Roman Catholic Priests* (1999, Greenwood) and *Sins Against the Innocents: Sexual Abuse by Priests and the Role of the Catholic Church* (Greenwood, 2004); co-author of *Getting Together, Staying Together: The Stanford University Course on Intimacy* (FirstBooks, 2000); and co-editor of *Faith and Health: Psychological Perspectives* (2001, Guilford). He conducts research concerning religious faith and health outcomes, the psychological benefits of exercise, and psychological issues among Catholic clergy. Over the course of his career, he has published more than 100 professional journal articles. Plante has appeared and been featured on the BBC, CNN, PBS's *News Hour with Jim Lehrer*, National Public Radio, and local television news shows as well as in national magazines and newspapers including *Time Magazine, US News and World Report, USA Today, Newsweek, the New York Time, the Los Angeles Times, the London Times,* and *the Washington Post.*

Some Other New Harbinger Titles

The Power of Two Workbook, Item 3341 $19.95

Adult Children of Divorce, Item 3368 $14.95

Fifty Great Tips, Tricks, and Techniques to Connect with Your Teen, Item 3597 $10.95

Helping Your Child with OCD, Item 3325 $19.95

Helping Your Depressed Child, Item 3228 $14.95

The Couples's Guide to Love and Money, Item 3112 $18.95

50 Wonderful Ways to be a Single-Parent Family, Item 3082 $12.95

Caring for Your Grieving Child, Item 3066 $14.95

Helping Your Child Overcome an Eating Disorder, Item 3104 $16.95

Helping Your Angry Child, Item 3120 $17.95

The Stepparent's Survival Guide, Item 3058 $17.95

Drugs and Your Kid, Item 3015 $15.95

The Daughter-In-Law's Survival Guide, Item 2817 $12.95

Whose Life Is It Anyway?, Item 2892 $14.95

It Happened to Me, Item 2795 $17.95

Act it Out, Item 2906 $19.95

Parenting Your Older Adopted Child, Item 2841 $16.95

Boy Talk, Item 271X $14.95

Talking to Alzheimer's, Item 2701 $12.95

Helping a Child with Nonverbal Learning Disorder or Asperger's Syndrome, Item 2779 $14.95

The 50 Best Ways to Simplify Your Life, Item 2558 $11.95

When Anger Hurts Your Relationship, Item 2604 $13.95

Call **toll free, 1-800-748-6273,** or log on to our online bookstore at **www.newharbinger.com** to order. Have your Visa or Mastercard number ready. Or send a check for the titles you want to New Harbinger Publications, Inc., 5674 Shattuck Ave., Oakland, CA 94609. Include $4.50 for the first book and 75¢ for each additional book, to cover shipping and handling. (California residents please include appropriate sales tax.) Allow two to five weeks for delivery.

Prices subject to change without notice.